C O

*To my mother, who in all ways
has helped me to embrace faith and
persevere beyond pain.*

TWENTY-THIRD PUBLICATIONS
A Division of Bayard
One Montauk Avenue, Suite 200
New London, CT 06320
(860) 437-3012 or (800) 321-0411
www.23rdpublications.com

ISBN 978-1-58595-786-6
Library of Congress Control Number: 2010938683
Printed in the U.S.A.

ACKNOWLEDGMENTS

This book was years in the making—years of pain and years of prayer. Throughout, God never abandoned me, nor did he allow his light to be extinguished, even in the darkest of times. For him and for all he is, I praise and thank him!

My thanks also go out to all who were instrumental in bringing this book to the hands of readers, especially the editorial and publication team at Twenty-Third Publications: Paul Pennick, Dan Connors, Gwen Costello, Dan Smart, Kerry Moriarty, Sue Cameron and Michelle Gerstel. Your presence and kindness are true blessings!

To the many people who have inspired me in my journey, as well as those who are mentors, prayer warriors, cherished family and friends, my heartfelt appreciation. A special note of thanks to cousins Carrie, Ed, and Kathy; friends Barbara, Carolyn, Veneice and Tony, Linda, Janet, Anne, Diana, Marilyn and Jean; the members of the American Behçet's Disease Association (www.behcets.com) and the ABDA board; Sean Herriott and Doug Johnson at Relevant Radio (www.relevantradio.com); Lisa Copen and Rest Ministries (www.restministries.com); Tom Norris, Marianne Muellerleile and the American Chronic Pain Association (www.theacpa.com); Carole Greene and Edmond Brosnan at Catholic News Service (www.catholicnews.com); and Francine Rivers, Leslie Sansone, Stephen Ray Mitchell, MD, Christina Puchalski, MD, Father Michael Alfano, Sister Rose Pacatte, Father Frank Desiderio, CSP, Father Chris Ponnet, Father Paul Bernadicou, SJ, and Father Germán Sánchez.

My doctors have been tremendous in their insight, care, patience, and support. Thanks so very much, especially, to David Hallegua, MD, Jay Schapira, MD, Kathryn Gardner, MD, and Kathleen Clemans, DDS.

Finally, to those who will read this book—thank you for journey-
ing with me a little ways. I hope that the time you spend with Job and
Jesus here will provide you with encouragement and sustenance for
your daily and nightly walk with pain. And may Our Lord's strength,
protection, compassion, and grace take you beyond the suffering and
into immense joy.

LOS ANGELES, JULY 2010

INTRODUCTION

Pain is one of life's most debilitating, depressing, and dark sensations. Chronic pain, relentless and ongoing, can make life seem almost unbearable. And when treatments aimed at alleviating pain do not work (or stop working), we can be plunged even deeper into a terrible place where the future seems more than bleak—it seems impossible.

Pain can wrench us away from everything we love—people, activities, even God.

Yes, it *can* wrench us away…*if* we let it.

At various times in my life, pain has stopped me in my tracks, isolated me from others, and made me wonder if a better day would ever come. Whether because of accidents (a hard suitcase falling on my head from an overhead compartment on an airplane, for example) or illness (lupus, knee osteoarthritis, scoliosis, and pleurisy, for example), pain has been a constant companion in my childhood and adult years—and I've now come to realize that it probably won't go away anytime soon.

That realization—that pain is always there—is not easy to accept. Who among us looks forward to day after day of feeling awful, not being able to move well, or, worse, not being able to move at all? Who relishes endless pain-racked nights or days of feeling like the world is racing by, leaving us stranded and alone?

Who wants to acknowledge that the lives God gives us are less than ideal?

As we chafe against the binding power of pain, we look to doctors for medications, to other people for sympathy, to God for relief. Some of us venture into perilous waters, experimenting with dangerous habits that inevitably lead to hopeless complications and even more pain.

1

We, in our humanness, cry to God for pity. We bargain ("I'll be a better person if you'll cure me of my pain"). We rail ("If you are bringing me such torment, then I don't believe in your love anymore"). We plead ("Please, Lord, take this pain away"). We put forth our case to God ("I've lived a good life. Why do you do this to me?") and expect an immediate reply.

We want to be happy—and pain-free. Only then, we may think, will life move ahead. Only then will we be capable of feeling joy.

It's only natural. When we are children, we recoil from things that can bring us pain. A sharp needle. A snarling dog. A hot stovetop.

We take our child-learned instincts to avoid pain and rely on them to shield us from harm as adults. We throw out food that has spoiled. We wait for traffic to clear before entering an intersection. We wear protective clothing against thorny, bristly growth in our gardens.

If we take such measures to protect ourselves from external threats, it's no wonder that we don't want the pain that resides inside our bodies.

Yes, we don't want it.

But it still is.

There isn't a person alive who will sail through his or her time on earth without physical or emotional pain or both. Some people will have more of it. Some will have it for a longer period of time. But all will have pain.

That's part of being human, too.

So, given that pain will be with us in some form from the beginning of our lives to the end, what do we really do about it?

Or, more to the point, how do we see beyond pain and allow our lives to sing with hope, faith, love, yes, and joy?

For more than a decade, I've been involved with patient advocacy and have met scores of wonderful people who live vibrant lives while experiencing harsh, painful physical challenges. These women, men, and children are not all gifted with incredible talent, nor are they all wealthy, highly educated, or socially secure. But each is an example of what someone can do when pain would be otherwise debilitating.

These shining lights have taught me so very much!

In this book, I hope to pass along what I and my fellow sufferers have learned about living beyond pain, shaping lives that are positive, productive, and potent with promise and faith.

This is not a book about curing pain. Each individual needs to consult with appropriate, competent medical professionals about diagnosing, monitoring, and treating pain and its causes.

This book is about what people in pain can do to contribute to the world around them, nurture love in themselves and others, and know their worth—great as it is—as precious members of God's grace-filled world.

This book is also about tying in our current suffering with faith, and seeing the holiness in our health challenges. It is a book about taking our life experience and bringing it into our communities in a very active, positive manner so that all may know greater compassion, respect, and appreciation for the pure gift of life.

Finally, this is a book based on two remarkable, pain-filled lives from Scripture: Job and Jesus.

﷽ Why Job?

As a newly diagnosed lupus patient, I was particularly drawn to the story of Job, the upright man whose life fell apart seemingly all at once. Job's losses parallel the losses that I and many people with pain experience, especially the lost connections with friends and loved ones who do not understand the place of suffering in life.

Indeed, with pain comes loss. First, there is loss of health. Then, there can be loss of movement, activity, employment, and position in society. Friends can stop calling. Family members can become impatient when the pain lingers day after day.

Faith can also start to slip away as pain takes over, which is why Job's story is even more compelling.

As Job's suffering increased, as his friends were railing away that he should be angry with God, Job clung to faith.

That's not to say that he didn't ask God questions. Nor did he ignore the utter horror of what his life had become.

But Job recognized that God was God and he himself was a mere human. Job acknowledged God's supremacy and accepted his lot in life, eventually striving to redeem himself and his friends and living an even more God-focused life after his ordeal than before.

Unshakable faith is a tall order when pain pummels our bodies.

But often, when we're like Job and stripped of everything else, faith is the only thing that remains to connect us with something beyond ourselves, beyond our trials, beyond pain.

The ending of the Book of Job is a remarkable turnabout, with Job's redemption affecting not only him but the very friends and family who were so problematic during his darkest days. I won't give it away here (I will talk about this in the book itself), but the way Job's life turned around illustrates clearly how physical and emotional ordeals can give us strength and wisdom to make a difference in others' lives—truly a way to see and act beyond pain.

ஃ Jesus, Human and Divine

The gospels sing of Jesus' miracles, parables, and compassion. They also describe the terrible emotional and physical suffering our Lord endured, which took him from the triumphant entry into Jerusalem, along the walk to Calvary and to death. Although it is easy to consider his death as the culmination of his suffering, Jesus' work did not end there. Rather, through his resurrection, Jesus not only ensured for us eternal salvation, but also demonstrated that, when undergone in faith, suffering leads to heaven.

Especially potent to me is Jesus' time in the Garden of Gethsemane, on the evening of his betrayal. We are told in Matthew (26:38) that Jesus said to Peter and the two sons of Zebedee, "My soul is sorrowful even to death." Jesus knew what was about to happen, and in his humanness, he felt the heavy burden of loss already weighing upon him. In a way, Jesus was showing us that it is all right to feel sorrow, sadness, even despair when faced with great personal suffering. All right, yes, and supremely human.

Next, Matthew tells us that Jesus "advanced a little and fell prostrate in prayer, saying, 'My Father, if it is possible, let this cup pass from me...'" (Matthew 26:39). Again, Jesus articulates what so many of us feel when we are in pain—we want so much for our suffering to stop, and we pray earnestly that it will.

But then Jesus arrives at the place to which we are also called. After asking for the cup to pass, Jesus concludes his prayer, "yet, not as I will, but as you will" (Matthew 26:39).

It is this surrender to God's will that takes the burden from our shoulders and allows us to move onward, even while the inevitable pain still festers.

And when we can move onward, wonderful and great things can happen—things like profound joy.

Joy?!

The more I live with pain, the more precious and present is my joy. When I speak of joy, I don't mean unbridled glee or complete and constant happiness.

To me, joy is the uplifting feeling of gratitude at all gifts, great and small, especially the pleasure of nurturing and helping others.

True, at times I might shout for joy or sing with joy, as described in Scripture. Usually, these outward expressions are because of a specific event—good news from a medical test, a friend's engagement or another milestone accomplished.

On a more consistent basis, however, my joy is more like that expressed by John the apostle when he writes, "Nothing gives me greater joy than to hear that my children are walking in the truth" (3 John 4).

I can imagine John sitting as he wrote, perhaps squinting in the feeble light of an oil lamp, scratching his words on crude paper, waving away the flies from his face, trying to ignore the rumble in his hungry stomach—and smiling as he envisioned those to whom he wrote thriving in the faith. For John, it didn't take mountains of money or fame to bring joy. Spreading the gospel was most important—and others' "walking in the truth" was most joy-giving.

When we live with terrible pain, we often cannot do the things we used to love to do. As we lament our failing health, we are prone to deeply mourn what we used to do and be. A certain amount of mourning is necessary in order to accept how life is now, but if we let our thoughts dwell too much and too long on where we used to be, we won't be able to dream about where we can go. And we certainly won't get there, either.

If John the apostle had thought only of the tremendous obstacles standing in the way of others' knowing Jesus, he would never have been able to witness as he did, reach the unreachable, and bring so many over to the Lord. By persevering as he did, he was able to achieve that glow of joy "greater" than any other.

We see this example of joy coming amidst and after enduring trials through many other people in the Bible: From Abraham and Sarah (imagine their joy after all those years waiting to welcome a son into their family!) to the Apostle Paul (who wrote so splendidly, "I am filled with encouragement, I am overflowing with joy all the more because of all our affliction" [2 Corinthians 7:4]). And, we see something else: Whether coming after, or co-existing with, pain, true joy does not simply abide—it acts.

So, Abraham and Sarah did more than admire their son, Isaac. They dedicated him to the Lord.

Paul did more than write of his joy. He infused his witness with it, drawing even more people to believe in Jesus.

After his ordeal, Job re-established his life of righteousness, extending his hand in goodness and mercy to others.

Jesus, through his suffering and death on the cross, fulfilled the promise made by his Father and granted us eternal salvation in the ultimate expression of love.

Yes, joy is a wonderful emotion of gratitude, elation, and celebration all rolled into one.

It is also a catalyst for action—the positive, powerful, inspirational kind of action that helps make the world better and brighter.

For Us, Then, Joy

If we believed there were no good reasons to even try to make something positive of our lives of pain, then we probably wouldn't. However, we know that there could be something better in life than dwelling on pain—or else we wouldn't ask to feel better. We wouldn't try this or that new treatment. We wouldn't wish that life were different.

The truth is that we know there is a better way to handle pain than to allow it to rule every aspect of our lives, dominate all conversations, and focus our attention completely on ourselves. To find that better way, we first have to accept both our lives in pain and the fact that there are things greater than ourselves—and such acceptance is not easy at all.

Not easy. But also not impossible. Job did it.

Jesus acknowledged his human emotions and lifted himself up to God the Father's will.

Each day, I am amazed by the number of people who live with terrible health situations—and do marvelous things in this world.

There's the woman, bedridden with deteriorating bones, who fellowships with others on the Internet.

There's the man with an inherited chronic illness who uses his example of faith to teach his daughter, who also has the condition, about the preciousness of life.

One older woman I know can barely walk, yet she prays every day for specific intentions she's gathered from friends and even total strangers.

The person who cannot speak, see, or hear teaches us to be compassionate and to bring Jesus into others' lives.

The person who creeps slowly with a walker down the grocery aisles teaches us about de-stressing and pacing ourselves.

How much we learn from others!

How much we can give others, too!

How much joy there is in the world and in our hearts—just waiting for us to uncover it, release it, and celebrate it!

In our society, the news media have become accustomed to pigeon-holing suffering into neat headlines and sound bites. For example, when a natural disaster occurs, affecting multitudes of people, the news is filled with the tragedy for perhaps two or three "news cycles." Poignant pictures grace nightly broadcasts and media websites. Then, other stories take the fore, and the pictures and people from the previous disaster fade from memory. Seldom is the same emphasis put on the initial tragedy weeks later—although those affected are still hurting greatly.

In our communities, too, there tends to be a flurry of giving at certain times of the year, especially in November and December. But come January, even when people are still needy and hungry, the flurry ends.

Television and advertisements offer myriad fixes for physical, emotional, and even some spiritual crises and illnesses. This has driven up an expectation that someone might suffer for a time—but, surely, not forever.

Those of us with chronic, painful conditions know otherwise. And yet, each of us has felt the sting of the question, "Aren't you over that yet?"

As if we're doing something wrong by still being ill or otherwise suffering!

As if we can't possibly have good lives as long as we are in pain.

Actually, the longer I've lived with pain, the more I realize that I, for one, can't sit around and wait for it to go away before I contribute to the world around me. Before I enjoy God's world and praise him for his gifts. Before I do what he put me on earth to do.

For me, it's vital that I see beyond the pain I experience daily so I can live life as God wants.

This doesn't mean that I push myself to feeling worse—"No pain, no gain" is not a slogan I adhere to. Rather, I've learned to accept my pain such as it is, do what I can to ensure that I don't aggravate it, and then fold those feelings into the rest of the day and night.

The activity that takes me out of my sphere of pain, that brings empathy, compassion, and positive caring into the outside world is activity that gives me greater energy, drive, faith, and hope. And joy.

There is no joy in letting pain sink so deep into me that I'm immobilized spiritually, emotionally, and physically.

But if I do even the smallest thing to contribute to the world beyond my pain, I kindle a joy that grows with each prayer raised, smile given, or encouraging e-mail sent.

If I lift up a hearty "thank you" to the Lord for the beauty of his world, I, too, am lifted up.

If I take a moment to find humor, I, too, will be tickled.

I pray that this book will lift you up, tickle you, and help you better understand that we who live with constant pain are not worthless. We are not victims of injustice and despair. We are not unloved.

Rather, there is much for us to do and be, given the lives we live. And there are many joys awaiting us, if we choose to reach out, look, hope and live…beyond pain.

Job did it.

Jesus did it.

You can, too!

O Lord, Father and Creator,
open my eyes to your wonderful works
and my ears to your powerful words.
For this time I spend now,
help me to focus, not on my pain,
but upon what I can learn.
And open my heart,
so that your peace may enfold me,
now and forever.
Amen.

Author's note: It is not necessary to have read the Book of Job and New Testament passages to which I refer in this book. However, you might want to review them for your own study as you read this work. All the Scripture passages quoted in this book are taken from the *New American Bible, the New Catholic Translation.*

JOB

The Everyperson
in All of Us

When I mentioned writing this book, almost everyone I spoke with thought they knew all about Job. On the surface, most people told me, his story could be summed up in the sentence, "When bad things happen to good people."

But in reading and re-reading Job, I realized there is much depth and nuance to the story that often goes unnoticed. Far more than disaster befalling the most righteous man in the world, Job is the story of someone human stumbling and then falling without a clear understanding of what is happening to him. Yes, bad things "happen to" Job, but he also contributes to the calamities by his actions and his attitude.

It is really only when he acknowledges how powerless he is that he starts to heal from the physical and emotional pain that assails him throughout the bulk of the story.

So, Job is not an inaccessible tale of a man who was completely in control of his life and wealth. He is like each of us, human and trying to do the right thing out of a flawed but faithful heart.

Another striking aspect of Job is the reaction of his friends when he falls terribly ill after losing all of his material wealth and most of his family. These friends encourage him to get angry and rail against God; they even criticize Job for how he's handling his situation.

These so-called friends certainly talk a lot! But just how true are such friends?

The parallels between Job's friends and our own are many—and tell another part of the story of how difficult it is to live with chronic, debilitating conditions. Sometimes, friends are our lifelines, the people who stand by us through everything. But sometimes, too, they are problematic.

God is, of course, central to the story of Job. But so often we forget about another actor in the drama—Satan. Yes, when we are in pain, we often heap all the blame on God. Do we consider that Satan might be trying to use our illness to break us away from God? Do we understand that how we cope with our pain and how we strive to stay close to God is more the point of our suffering than the actual physical toll it takes?

Job's story gives us much insight into these and other aspects of our life with pain—and how to get past it through acceptance and will.

But, before going into all of these, we first must begin at the beginning...

Father in heaven,
bless this time I spend with you,
so that I may truly listen
in your presence.
Help me to see what you
would have me see
and not what I believe,
in my humanness,
to be true.
Amen.

A Life Gone Awry

*In the land of Uz, there was a
blameless and upright man named Job,
who feared God and avoided evil.*

THE BOOK OF JOB 1:1

For people who have experienced a catastrophic illness, trauma, or accident and are still racked with horrible pain, life "before" often takes on a rosy hue, as if everything had been perfect. Life "after" becomes a hated ordeal that we resent all the more because it takes us further away from our Edenic life "before."

As our problems and pain increase, we may draw an even greater distinction between "before" and "after." Not only was our life better "before," but the world around us was better, too. Loved ones didn't have annoying habits. Work wasn't onerous at all. Traffic flowed. Life was one big vacation.

Or was it?

Although there were many good things about our lives before pain, there were many not-so-good things, too. No one is perfect. We are, after all, human, and being human means that there will be good and bad, joyful and painful times throughout.

14

It's no accident (pardon the pun) that The Book of Job begins with his "life before." The writer wanted us to see Job as someone who appeared to do everything correctly and was reaping great rewards. In the first verse of chapter 1, we meet a man who not only enjoys the respect of his community, but who also is a man of faith. We meet someone "blameless and upright," and very wealthy. Besides his seven sons and three daughters, Job's livestock was so numerous that "he was greater than any of the men of the East" (Job 1:3).

There are people like this today, people, perhaps in your church, who, on the surface, seem to have everything going for them. Fine car. Beautiful family. Honored position within the congregation. Money with which to buy nice things and tithe abundantly.

Perfect?

Remember, these people who exude prosperity are human, too. As we learn from Job, no one's life is completely perfect.

> [Job's sons] used to take turns giving feasts, sending invitations to their three sisters to eat and drink with them. And when each feast had run its course, Job would send for them and sanctify them, rising early and offering holocausts for every one of them. For Job said, "It may be that my sons have sinned and blasphemed God in their hearts." This Job did habitually.   ❧ JOB 1:4–5

Although Job lived honorably, it would appear that his children were eager party-goers, and perhaps worse.

How perfect could Job's life be if his children did not seem to share his faith and observance of temperance?

How perfect could Job himself be, if he seemed, in our modern-day terminology, to be an "enabler," someone who cleaned up the mess his children made, without holding them accountable for it?

I can imagine this concerned father fretting over the exploits of his sons by night and hurrying to offer holocausts the next day so that

God would not be angry with them. Today, we see this same behavior in our own homes and in society at large. The mother who refuses to admit to a child's drug use. The father who consistently bails out his child financially. The friend who turns a blind eye to another's sexual promiscuity.

In a way, we might say that Job's first failing was to deny the pain around him and in his life, and try to keep up appearances with his community and with God.

The conversation between God and Satan puts this in clearer terms: God applauds Job for being so devout, but Satan argues that Job is that way simply because God has made Job's life so easy.

> [Satan tells God,] "You have blessed the work of his hands, and his livestock are spread over the land. But now put forth your hand and touch anything that he has and surely he will blaspheme you to your face."   JOB 1:10–11

No life is completely bereft of good things. In fact, sometimes when we are in great pain, we place extra emphasis and attention on those things that bring us even a little happiness.

- Do you recognize the good things in your life?

- Do you take them for granted?

- Have you ever said, "I'd fall apart if I ever lost
  _____"?

- Are your affections for things justified?

The Lord gives Satan leave to bring trouble upon Job, to test Job's loyalty, with one condition: God says, "do not lay a hand upon his person" (Job 1:12).

Satan begins to ruin Job's life, giving Job, in every sense, a really bad day. On one day, Job's herds are stolen and his herdsmen are slain, lightning falls from heaven and consumes his flocks of sheep and their shepherds, Chaldeans steal Job's camels and slay those tending them, and, finally, Jobs' sons and daughters are killed when a great wind rips down the house in which they are partying (Job 1:13–20).

Job's reaction to these events is immediate and very human. He "began to tear his cloak and cut off his hair. He cast himself prostrate upon the ground…" (Job 1:20). But then, after venting his profound emotional pain, Job speaks words of faith:

> "Naked I came forth from my mother's womb
> and naked shall I go back again.
> The Lord gave and the Lord has taken away;
> blessed be the name of the Lord!"
>
> ❧ JOB 1:21

Often, when we are in severe pain or have just received terrible news, our first reaction is like Job's. In our own way, we physically express our pain, we cry out, throw things (hopefully not breakable things, and not at anyone else!). We externalize the horrible feelings hurting us inside by crying, dropping to out knees, slamming doors.

We might lash out at someone nearby.

We might spew hatred against God.

Job's words, spoken after his display of anguish, show us another way to bring anger into focus and start to heal. Instead of condemning or berating God for bringing terrors upon him and his children, Job remembers the good things that God has given him, and he praises God. Job acknowledges God's might: Just as God gives good things, God can take them away, too. Job also says, very perceptively, that nothing really belonged to him in the first place.

> "Naked I came forth from my mother's womb,
> and naked shall I go back again."

Job's words fly in the face of our modern consumerism. We buy, own, sell, borrow, and lend often without thinking deeply about what we are doing. Not that it's wrong to possess material goods or feel a sense of loyalty to others. But, if we let our possessiveness rule our feelings, we lose sight of the One who makes all possible for us.

Over the past several years, we have seen moving broadcasts of people whose homes and lives have been devastated by natural disaster. These people have experienced deep pain and suffer greatly, even after the floods or fires are gone. But time and time again, out of the churning waters or ashes comes remarkable resolve to rebuild those lives beaten down and to acknowledge, like Job, that things may come and go. Only God, with his love, is everlasting.

Expressing anguish is an important step in healing from hurt and pain. But just as important is recognizing that we need God in our corners, however dark that corner may be.

We might still have tears streaming down our faces and fists clenched in anger. But if we can get to the point where we speak those stunning words from Job, where we can praise God for being God, we can begin to move away from what is holding us back and toward strength and resolve.

Chapter 1 of the Book of Job ends with the phrase, "In all this Job did not sin, nor did he say anything disrespectful of God" (Job 1:22).

Job survives the first test carried out by Satan!

But he, for all the things and people he has lost, has not been stricken physically.

Yet.

In Job, chapter 2, God and Satan talk over Job's loyalty to the Lord. God is impressed with Job's steadfastness. Satan, however, is not impressed.

"Skin for Skin! All that a man has will he give for his life...," Satan says, "But now put forth your hand and touch his bone and his flesh, and surely he will blaspheme you to your face" (Job 2:4–5).

God allows Satan to torment Job, exhorting "only, spare his life" (Job 2:6).

> Pain can lead us to try to bargain with God, offering to do or be something in exchange for a lessening or ending of pain. But deep down, we know that bargaining with God doesn't work.
>
> • Do you bargain with God about your pain?
>
> • Do you put conditions on your faith?

Job is made to suffer severe boils "from the soles of his feet to the crown of his head" (Job 2:7). Not only is this horribly painful, it is also a condition that would, in Jewish society at the time, render Job "unclean," a pariah and social outcast.

Today, those with visible disabilities might relate to Job's affliction and subsequent "unclean" status. Many times, I've heard from people in wheelchairs, or who use walkers, canes, guide dogs, or other visible signs of disability, that some people will look away, not speak to them, or otherwise shut them off from polite conversation. Even in worship, there might be subtle barriers to the disabled fully participating in community services—stairs leading up to the altar, for example, make it impossible for wheelchair-bound individuals to go there.

Public ostracism happens to those with invisible disabilities, too. One lupus patient I know was participating in a yard sale to benefit lupus research. Two women approached. Just as one of them was going to pick up one of the items for sale, the other stopped her, saying, "Don't touch that! These people have lupus! It's contagious."

Lupus is not contagious at all. But even the perception that a person has it does make some people run the other way.

Negative reactions to people with disabilities can build thick walls between otherwise good people. As someone in pain, you are the ideal individual to help others understand your desire to live a life beyond the pain you suffer. You can educate others so that you and they can better live out a Christ-centered witness.

- Can you think of one situation where you feel isolated because of your disability and pain? Is your church accessible, for example? Do you want to be part of a prayer group, but the church-based ones are impossible for you to attend?

- Can you come up with three ways in which you can help the able-bodied include you in activities? Pray by phone, for example, or incorporate your movement challenges into a service.

As Job's pain continues and he feels more of the social effects of his affliction, his wife encourages him to rail against God.

"Still holding to your innocence?" she asks. "Curse God and die" (Job 2:9).

But still acknowledging God's greatness, Job says, "We accept good things from God; and should we not accept evil?" (Job 2:10).

There is hope behind Job's words. In harking back to the good, Job calls up memories of "life before," and the pleasure that was there. His praise of God earlier, however, gives way to a question, reflecting his fragile emotions:

"Should we not accept evil?"

As medication fails, as people abandon us and the agonizing days lengthen, we doubt God's abiding love. We fall deeper into pain, depression, and loneliness.

Yet, hope is a light for us, a beacon to steer us through dark waters and bring us to shore, if we choose to embrace it.

- What prayers bring you hope? (Musical prayers, prayers from childhood, prayers of thanks)

- With what good can you surround yourself so that you may see light even in your darkness? (Pictures of loved ones or a special place, inspiring stories, Scripture verses that speak of Christ's love for us)

Acceptance of physical fragility is a difficult process and not one that happens all at once. For someone whose life "before pain" was full, fairly happy, and healthy, accepting a new and difficult life can seem impossible. Job's question reflects the two-edged sword of acceptance: If we do not accept our pain, we cannot move beyond it. But if we do accept it, are we in some way giving in or being weak?

Some of the most useful bridges to help us reconcile the "after" with the "before" are the good relationships we have with family and friends. Sometimes, it takes a good friend to sit down with us and "talk turkey," that is, help us see that we cannot escape from our "now," but we can still have a life of meaning.

Toward the end of chapter 2, three of Job's good friends hear of his troubles and journey to "give him sympathy and comfort" (Job 2:11). Their visit reveals the complexity of relationships, especially when one person is living with the burden of pain, and offers insight into being honest, faithful, and caring—in unexpected ways!

O Lord,
my life seems to be
one long succession of broken dreams,
physical torment,
and relationships destroyed.
Help me to fix my eyes on you,
my mind on that which is good,
and my strength on doing my best
to live a life that is pleasing to you.
Amen.

Friends and Family

*For mischief comes not out of the earth,
nor does trouble spring out of the ground; But man
himself begets mischief as sparks fly upward.*

JOB 5:6–7

One of the most common complaints that I hear from people living with pain is that they are so very lonely. I understand this—pain can be an isolating condition for many reasons. Perhaps, for example, someone cannot move about easily and so does not attend social events or even Mass on Sunday. Perhaps someone is afraid that reaching out to others will be too taxing on precious energy or, worse, that the sufferer will experience another deep pain—the pain of rejection.

When I look from the outside in, that is, when I try to put myself in the shoes of a healthy person, I think I understand, too, how difficult it is to keep a relationship going with someone whose whole world seems so very different from "normal." People in pain have different priorities than those who are hale, and people who are healthy are able to move about mentally and physically with more agility and speed. Truly, the "inner clock" of a person in pain moves at a much slower pace than that of the outside world!

But as hard as it is to establish and maintain good relationships with others, and given the many obstacles that seem to prevent true, deep friendships from taking root, we know from the earliest pages of Genesis to the New Testament letters of St. Paul that God did not intend for us to live on this earth in a friendless, relationship-less bubble. We have gifts that are meant to be shared with others.

Good relationships lift us up and make us feel love and give love: They reflect the love and care of Christ. If we did not reach out to others, we would not be fulfilling our promise and purpose as witnesses to Christ.

So, how do we overcome the difficulties a life of pain poses in order to forge healthy relationships? Is it possible that we who suffer might be the ones who "make mischief" and stand in the way of establishing and building supportive, uplifting friendships?

The greatest tool we have to build lasting bonds is the gift of communication. What we say to others, and how we say it, sets the tone for friendships. We can glean tremendous insight from Job's experience communicating with his friends.

When his friends first see Job in his distress, they are shaken to the core. Instead of the healthy, prosperous, strong man they have known, they find someone they do not recognize. Their immediate reaction is one of horror, a natural reaction when we see someone we love suffer so deeply. I experienced similar reactions when I began to lose all of my hair, one of the first symptoms that my immune system was in overdrive, which eventually brought me to a diagnosis of lupus. My ponytail became thinner and thinner, and soon it was impossible to hide the widening bald spots on my scalp. Those close to me looked worried, asked questions, were as confused as I.

Experiencing terrible pain might not be as visible in the person suffering as was my loss of hair. (Balding women do stand out in a crowd!) But as pain takes hold of our lives, other things can visibly reflect our downward spiral. A cluttered, dusty house, for example.

Unpaid bills. Unanswered telephone calls. A pile of unread newspapers. An unkempt yard.

Perhaps pain gets so bad that the effort to dress each day is too much, and we don't bother to get out of the bulky robe and slippers, shower, or brush our teeth. Or, we might not even get out of bed except for the most necessary of activities.

A loved one who sees us in this state of disarray might react like Job's friends, to a lesser or greater extent, and be aghast at how we seem to have deteriorated. They may be speechless, at first.

Job's friends are unable to speak when they first see him. In fact, they "sat down upon the ground with him seven days and seven nights, but none of them spoke a word to him; for they saw how great was his suffering" (Job 2:13).

Seven days and seven nights!

Job must wonder why his friends don't say anything. He must have expected them to offer words of comfort, encouragement, or, well, something.

Perhaps irritated that his friends are speechless, Job is the one who finally talks. But he doesn't thank them for coming to his side, and he doesn't speak of their sacrifice of time and travel. No, he launches into a speech lamenting his own suffering.

> "Perish the day on which I was born,
>   the night when they said, 'The
>   child is a boy!'
> May that day be darkness;
>   let not God above call for it,
>   nor light shine upon it!"
>   *ֶ* JOB 3:2

As he speaks, his complaints increase:

"For sighing comes more readily to
    me than food,
    and my groans well forth like water...
I have no peace nor ease;
    I have no rest for trouble comes!"
        JOB 3:24, 26

Does the presence of Job's friends bring him any comfort at all?

If I put myself in Job's friends' shoes, I think I would be slightly...
okay, perhaps more than slightly...irritated that my effort at lending
support was being disregarded or unnoticed. And indeed, Job's friend
Eliphaz reflects this same emotion in his first speech.

Eliphaz begins by saying, "If someone attempts a word with you,
will you mind?" (Job 4:1).

He then reminds Job of some of the things he did for others, before he fell into such suffering, asking how Job can possibly com-

Living with pain is a raw, rough experience. Between
the wretched state of our bodies and the clinical way
many medical professionals view us, it can be easy to
forget the more polite side of living, where courtesy and
manners still have a place. Yet, if we take the time to
practice being polite, we can begin to establish a sense
of respect and appreciation for others that can make us
better people—and better friends.

• What does it mean to you to be a good friend/spouse/
  child/parent?

plain so much when he has encouraged others to be strong and have faith.

Eliphaz says,

> "Behold, you have instructed many,
>   and have made firm their feeble hands…
> But now that it comes to you, you
>   are impatient…
> Is not your piety a source of confidence
>   and your integrity of life your hope?"
>
>   ﻻ JOB 4:3, 5, 6

I cannot help but think of the directive to "practice what we preach." This maxim is important to those of us who wish to reach out to others and be a friend, as much as to have friends. How much we respect those who follow their own advice! How greatly do we tend to dismiss those who tell others what to do or how to act, but don't behave the same way themselves!

- Are there times when you have forgotten to be polite to a friend or other loved one who makes the effort to visit with you?

- When you start a conversation with a friend, are you thinking of your condition first? Is what you say at first all about you?

- Do you expect comfort and support from friends and neglect to offer it to them?

Our attitude toward a life of pain speaks volumes about
how diligently we strive to live out our faith. When we
tell someone about how we are feeling, how we express
our situation also speaks about how we bear the cross
of pain. So, it is important to respond truthfully when
someone asks how we are doing. But it is also important to understand that there are many different ways of
expressing the same thing—and our underlying attitude
makes all the difference!

- What words do I use to describe my level and type
  of pain? Are there other ways that I could explain to
  someone how I am feeling?

- Do I use my words to push others away, or try to pun-
  ish them verbally as a way of expressing my anger
  over being in pain?

Throughout the rest of his first speech, Eliphaz tries to convince Job
that suffering is a way to witness to God's healing and power.

> Happy is the man whom God reproves!
>   The Almighty's chastening do not reject.
> For he wounds, but he binds up;
>   he smites, but his hands give healing.   JOB 5:17–18

He also tells Job what he, Eliphaz, would do were he in Job's shoes.

> "In your place, I would appeal to God,
>   and to God I would state my plea."   JOB 5:8

Job doesn't appreciate Eliphaz's advice. He complains anew about his suffering, and then directly criticizes his friend:

> "Have I no helper,
>   and has advice deserted me?
> A friend owes kindness to one in despair,
>   though he have forsaken the fear
>   of the Almighty."
>
> 🍎 JOB 6:13–14

We can empathize with Job's desire to have his friend agree completely with him. In our own lives, we sometimes crave the same kind of validation from friends and family members. We might confuse a loved one's agreeing with our anger at God or being despondent over our pain as obviously right and fitting.

But does this kind of attitude help us move beyond our pain, or does it dig us in further in a focus on self-pity?

- If our friends only parrot what we lament, are we really building trusting, truthful relationships?

- Who are the friends or family members whose advice you most appreciate, even if it goes against what you want to hear? How can you better nurture these relationships?

Perhaps Job responds to Eliphaz so sharply because he knows his friend is speaking truthfully, and the truth hurts. I had a similar experience a few months ago.

A person e-mailed me about an article I had written about ways to cope with chronic pain. The e-mail crackled with anger. The writer said I obviously did not understand living with pain because if I did, I could never suggest that someone should try to cope with it by using techniques such as singing, laughing, or other similar activities!

In reading the rest of the e-mail, I realized that the writer was not so much angry with me as with having to live with horrible pain. I prayed over how to respond, and finally did, gently pointing out that I do live with pain and explaining why I had suggested the activities in the article.

Another time, I was giving a talk at a book-signing one evening when a woman in the back of the room held up her hand and said, "Oh, I saw the book title [*Peace in the Storm: Meditations on Chronic Pain and Illness*], but I didn't realize this was about God. I'm an atheist. I don't need God or anyone else to help me with my illnesses. I can do it all on my own."

In the audience were several people of faith, including practicing Catholics. A few of the attendees began to question the woman, as did I, about just how deep her conviction was that she didn't need anyone. After a lengthy discussion, it became clear to me (and those gathered) that she really did rely on friends, health care professionals, and the life lessons imparted to her by her now-deceased parents. Clearly, she was not doing it all "on her own." Perhaps her anger was more due to consternation about the inherent contradiction between what she was declaring and what was really true in her life?

After Eliphaz speaks, Bildad chimes in. He laces his comments with humor, beginning with:

> "How long will you [Job] utter such things?
> The words from your mouth are like a mighty wind!"
>   JOB 8:2

Then, he assures Job that, although his current state is dire, his previous faith and God's justice and care, will restore him in the end. He refers to Job's "before" as a template for the future.

The element of humor that Bildad introduces reminds us of the importance of this gift in our lives, no matter how much pain we may be suffering. Sometimes, laughter is the thing that helps us rise above our pain, and laughter shared with a loved one is a blessing we too often forget to employ.

My first column for Catholic News Service was about the medical and emotional benefits of laughter through a program at UCLA Medical Center called RxLaughter. One of the program's first studies looked at whether children undergoing painful chemotherapy could benefit from exposure to something funny before their treatments. One group of children watched cartoons before undergoing chemo, while another did not. The study found that those children who had a good laugh before their treatment were more resilient and able to tolerate the chemo better than those who had not been exposed to the cartoons.

Laughter, even gentle chuckling, releases certain hormones associated with feelings of well-being and joy. It is also, by the way, wonderful exercise for "core" muscles and lungs! It's a gift from God.

- Do you feel it's impossible for you to laugh?

- Who is the person in your life who almost always makes you smile? How can you nurture this relationship more?

- What else can you do to encourage your sense of humor?

When we laugh with someone, we create a bond that transcends present suffering. Job's icy anger melts a little when he responds after Bildad's more gentle speech. His next speech is still filled with sadness-laced complaint, but also with questions for God.

Job wonders, "Why then did you bring me forth from the womb?" (Job 10:18).

In the midst of our suffering, we, too, might ask God "why?" It is a very human question, but not a very productive one. As Job's third friend, Zophar, says,

> "Can you penetrate the designs of God?
> Dare you vie with the perfection of the Almighty?"
>   ᔓ JOB 11:7

In other words, who are we to question God's reasoning? And, does our dwelling on this question help us along our faith-centered journey or does it prevent us from reaching a more holy state of being?

Job resents Zophar's challenge. After Zophar tries to get him to accept his humanness and his pain, Job begins his retort with:

> "No doubt you are the intelligent folk,
> And with you wisdom shall die!"
>   ᔓ JOB 12:2

He is angry that others, less righteous than he has been, seem to escape pain in their lives. He puts forth his "case" that with the good life he has lived prior to suffering, he should be spared from his present trials.

Job's arguments are impassioned, articulate, even at times poetic. But they still dig him further into living in the past and chafing against the present. They also reflect an unwillingness to submit to God's supremacy.

In the presence of three good, solid friends, Job still cannot let go of his own ego and allow God to fashion in him a new heart, stronger and more brilliant than "before." As we see in the second Cycle of Speeches, Job's resistance leads him not forward and to a better frame of mind, but rather deeper down—deep in the mire of suffering.

O Lord,
You are greater than I could ever imagine,
and your ways are beyond my understanding.
Help me rest in the comfort
that you love me, care about me,
and are guiding me toward
newness of spirit
and strength of faith
now and forever.
Amen.

Deep in the Mire

[Job said]: "He breaks me down on every side,
And I am gone; My hope he has uprooted like a tree."

JOB 19:10

Have you ever slogged through a field of mud? At first, the way might seem passable, but as you lift one foot after the other, the glue-like earth becomes stickier and sticker, the way more and more difficult. Each step becomes harder, and your efforts more intense.

If it's a big field of thick mud, you're probably completely exhausted by the time you take your last step in the mire.

In the Second Cycle of Speeches, Job's friends persist in trying to get him to accept his suffering and be strong through faith. Job's responses still reflect the sting of his suffering and his disappointment in God and his friends' seeming lack of sympathy.

But as the Book of Job goes on and Job's fight continues, changes in his demeanor reflect the toll that self-centered frustration and anger take.

First, Job grows "exhausted and stunned" (Job 16:7).

Today's medical research recognizes more profoundly the role that stress plays in exacerbating pain and many kinds of illness. Physically,

34

stress can tense already painful muscles and joints, raise blood pressure, and manifest itself in rashes, muscle spasms, and other symptoms.

Emotionally, stress can bring on extreme anxiety, affect mood, and result in an inability to cope reasonably with problems, responsibilities, and other people.

Anger is one emotion recognized as extremely stress-inducing, especially if it is prolonged and unchecked. Anger, and its close kin resentment, can be the proverbial salt in the wound for someone suffering from chronic, deep pain.

Anger is a very real way to isolate yourself from God and others. It is also an emotion that can sap energy, stress the body, and exacerbate pain.

- How do you handle anger? How can you handle it better?

- Have you ever considered that, when you are angry with God for not taking away your pain, your anger might be encouraging Satan?

There are myriad resources for coping with stress, including books, DVDs, exercise programs, support networks, and counselors and coaches, not to mention a plethora of anti-anxiety medications. But for these to be of significant help, we must understand that no life is completely free of stress, and that so much of coping with stress is our responsibility. For example, how we spend our time is, to a great extent, within our sphere of control.

Job's speeches to his friends, for example, leave no room for much else. He is exhausting himself by parrying his friends' suggestions. He dwells on his suffering to the point that he does not seem to be able to recall with gratitude his past accomplishments, or make any plans for future positive activities.

The longer Job slogs through the mire of self-pity, the greater his risk of completely alienating those around him, including his three stalwart friends.

In our own lives, the more we sit and dwell on our suffering, the more we risk convincing ourselves that suffering is all we have. And, if that is the case, we close out other people and God from offering us any solace.

We might also sabotage our own opportunities, setting ourselves up to fail so that we validate what we thought we believed—that our lives are hopeless. For example, we might set unrealistic goals for weight loss, daily chores, or other tasks because unconsciously we don't believe we can achieve them anyway.

Coping with pain is a daily struggle, not so much against the pain itself, but against ourselves and our tendency to give in to the pain rather than forge ahead.

"Before" pain and illness, goals were a natural part of life, whether in work, school, or personal pursuits. "After," with pain at the forefront, setting goals becomes more difficult, especially if health is unpredictable. So that we do not lose heart, goal-setting for the pain sufferer is more effective when it is reasonable and realistic—it might take longer to accomplish a long-held dream, but even the tiniest of steps can add up to achievement!

Another emotion that can cause undo stress is jealousy.

Several times, Job expresses resentment at his able-bodied friends and even people he does not know who seem prosperous and pain-free. Once again, as he slogs through this part of the mire of pain, he cannot seem to lift himself up and understand that he, too, was once prosperous and hale. Being human means that at times life will be easy, and at times it will not.

In our own lives, jealousy can manifest itself in many ways, none of them productive. We might lash out at a friend who has reason to celebrate—or we might not even acknowledge that person's achievement or good fortune.

We might hear of someone's success and automatically think, "Why isn't that me instead of him?" Or, "I know that she doesn't deserve to be so healthy; she smoked and drank and abused her body, where I did none of these things."

We might totally disregard the positive things in our own lives (just as Job disregards the loyalty and care of his friends), because they don't seem to be as good as what we perceive others to have.

- Are you so angry and frustrated that you set yourself up to fail?

- Do you have a cherished dream you think is unattainable now? Why? Are there creative ways you can take your dream, divide it up into small steps, and still pursue it?

- Have you accomplished anything since your pain became overwhelming? Have you celebrated your achievements? It's never too late!

> Jealousy can eat away at our gratitude and self-worth, as well as cause rifts between us and God.
>
> - Do I recognize the positive things in my life, or do I focus on others' lives and resent the things they have?
>
> - Do my jealous feelings leave a bitter taste in my mouth and heart, poisoning my ability to find comfort?

Like anger, jealousy is a negative emotion that is counterproductive to our ability to accept our lives and make the most of them moving forward. It does no good to covet another's lifestyle or possessions; rather, it leaves us deeper in the mire of self-pity, self-loathing, and anger that cuts to our soul.

In addition to fatigue, resentment, and astonishment, Job also experiences profound sadness: "Therefore am I dismayed before him" (Job 23:18).

Depression is a very real and serious aspect of living with chronic pain. Besides the ever-present specter of days and nights laced with suffering, life stresses (divorce, marriage, moving, job changes) can contribute to depression, as can certain medications and underlying health problems. Fortunately, there are treatments for depression and there is much more public understanding of the problem. Yes, there is help, if the patient chooses to seek it.

As with managing anger, coping with depression requires a willingness to step out of the mire of self and reach out to others—friends, family, clergy, or medical professionals who can, in turn, provide support and treatment. The person suffering needs to acknowledge that he or she cannot "do it all" alone.

Depression can be subtle or very overt. Signs of depression include excessive sleeping, feelings of helplessness and sadness, frequent crying, loss of interest in formerly enjoyable activities, and thoughts of death and/or suicide. When a person is depressed, he or she can easily feel that life is hopeless. Today, with the variety of treatments for the many forms of depression, there is more hope than ever before for someone suffering from depression. There is no shame in seeking help.

- Has anyone you know suggested that you might be depressed?

- Do you feel as if a dark cloud is shadowing your ability to be happy?

- Are you afraid to seek treatment for depression?

Although his three friends insist that God is supreme—no one can know the ways of the Lord, nor bargain or reason with him as with another person. But Job persists in professing his innocence and insists that God acknowledge this and restore him to his "flourishing days" (Job 29:4).

By now, we can see how tiresome Job's stubbornness has become to his friends and probably to those reading about him. He keeps saying the same thing over and over again—and getting nowhere except deeper in the mire. He views his past as some kind of perfect life, free of problems and full of prosperity and glory. He questions why God should bring him to such a difficult life, when he has lived blamelessly, and he ends his final speech with a simple yet forceful command to the Lord: "This is my final plea; let the Almighty answer me!" (Job 31:37).

I frequently hear from people who say they just wish God would talk to them, answer their questions, tell them what the purpose of their lives and suffering is. Indeed, it would be wonderful if we could all have what I call a "Moses Moment," where God's voice suddenly booms into our place of prayer and tells us, in our native language, what we wanted to know. How easy it would be to follow God's commands then!

But most of us will never have a bona fide Moses Moment. Most of us, when we pray, will think we hear only silence or perhaps a faint, unintelligible whisper.

Still, God is not mute. Sometimes, we think we do not hear him because we're too busy talking, complaining, crying out, or just making noise. Sometimes, too, we don't like the answer God gives, and we seek to override it.

We try to be what we wish God would be for us, and we thereby miss completely who God really is.

Another man sits with Job and his friends, and until now he has been silent. When Job commands that God answer him, the man, Elihu, cannot be silent any longer. His words reveal much about where Job and his friends are still going wrong—and his energy and conviction inspire a resolution to the entire, troubled story.

O Lord,
I know I have become so absorbed in my pain
that I have lost sight of who you are.
Help me in my struggle to
overcome my selfishness,
and lead me to greater comfort and knowledge
that you are in control over all.
Amen.

Talking Sense

Then Elihu proceeded and said:
"Do you think it right to say,
'I am just rather than God?'"

JOB 35:1-2

Most of us know at least one person who is blatantly, sometimes brutally, honest, a person who cuts to the core of an argument or problem. A person who talks sense amid all the nonsense.

Job knows such a person, and after his three friends fail to sway Job from his pedestal of self-pity, anger, and resentment, "sense talker" Elihu steps in and takes them all on.

As far as Elihu is concerned, Job and his three friends are gravely at fault: Job for his stubbornness and belief that God is wrong and he is right, and Eliphaz, Bildad, and Zophar because they haven't been forceful enough to speak the truth about God and Job's egotistical rants.

Not that Elihu speaks rashly. Until chapter 32, we are told that he has held back while the others talked because he is the youngest and wanted to wait for the "wisdom" of his elders to kick in. But after they've all had their turns talking (and in Elihu's view, talking in circles), Elihu is angry and has to jump in.

Elihu's eloquent speech has two major points: First, God is om-
nipotent and hears Job's prayers, but it is useless to try to force God's
hand for an answer or ease from suffering: "The case is before [God];
with trembling should you [Job] wait upon him" (Job 35:14).

Second, Elihu states simply that God is great and Job's understanding is small. Because God created the world and has rule over all,
people should be accountable to God, not the other way around.

> "The Almighty! We cannot discover him,
> 　　pre-eminent in power and judgment;
> 　His great justice owes no one an accounting.
> Therefore men revere him,
> 　　though none can see him, however
> 　　　wise their hearts."
> 　　 📖 JOB 37:23–24

When we live with daily and nightly pain, we so desperately want to
feel relief. We might expect God to cure us, for the same reasons Job
did, because we lived a prosperous, righteous life "before pain." Or we
might regard relief as "good" and pain as "bad," giving these conditions moral equivalents that lead us to think, erroneously, that God is
truly not a loving but a vengeful Father.

Elihu is trying to get Job to understand that, by the very nature of
our humanity, our lives will have both suffering and freedom from
suffering. As Job's friends tried to convince him, with less force of argument than Elihu, how we react to the suffering we experience, and
what we do with our lives from that point, is what truly matters.

What we do in the "darkness," then, is as important as what we do
in the light.

As Job did, we might think of our lives "before pain" as filled with unending happiness, when everything worked perfectly and those around us loved us unconditionally. So, now that we are suffering, we might think it is impossible to be happy, to even smile, again. (Some people have even told me that it physically hurts for them to smile and laugh!)

Before you decide that your life of pain is completely devoid of any hint of happiness, consider these questions:

- To you, does being happy only mean being pain-free? Or, can you think of other things, people, or memories that evoke feelings of happiness within you?

- Are you afraid that, if you appear happy, people might not take your suffering seriously? Are you afraid that, if you laugh at anything regarding your pain, people might think you are mentally unstable?

- Were there truly no times "before pain" when you were not happy?

- Are you relying on God or other people to make you happy, or to provide you with the things that make you happy?

Elihu's second observation is especially pertinent to Job, and to us. For a long time, Job has either sat silently (it took him seven days, remember, before he said anything to his three friends) or sat and complained, bargained, and pleaded with God.

What did Job really do during this time?

He made himself "weary," snapped at his friends, dwelt on what he viewed as a completely rosy past (leaving out the parts about his children's transgressions, his own enabling, and other less-than-rosy aspects). Job also became bitter and jealous of others.

What Elihu offers to Job is a way out of the mire, a way to action beyond his pain. Elihu reflects on God's greatness, and he suggests that Job "stand and consider the wondrous works of God!" (Job 37:14). In other words, do something positive instead of wallowing in your own mire!

Difficult words to hear, but spoken like a true friend!

In our own lives, if we are lucky, we have cultivated good friends who will comfort us in our time of need and also give us a swift verbal "kick" when we are becoming too self-absorbed. Oh, we might not like what our friend says; the pull of self-pity is very strong. But we know that unless we shake off what's holding us down, we'll find only more ways to feel unhappy and thoroughly useless. We might also develop jealousy toward the very friends who are so good for us, and we might self-sabotage other aspects of our lives that are, truly, positive and good.

Between lupus brain fog, which can zap my short- and long-term memory, and constant pain, which can make it difficult to concentrate on the day's schedule, I have become a big proponent of lists. Long lists. Short lists. Lists on little scraps of paper, or on legal-length pads. Wherever I put them, my daily lists are helpful not only for remembering the things I must do, but also the things I strive to accomplish. Sometimes, I don't complete everything I thought I should, and sometimes I get

Some people who contact me say that no one cares about them anymore and that they cannot rely on family or friends for comfort, let alone sage advice. My heart aches for each of these people; it is so very painful to feel you are alone. Yet, I also feel a sense of frustration when I consider these people live in the same world I do.

The person who is truly alone is really very rare.

There are loving, caring individuals in many corners of our lives—at church, our physicians' offices, our neighbors, our family members. What causes the sense of alienation is usually more complex than just a void of presence. Often, the sense of being alone has to do with the sufferer's overwhelming pain and difficulty in reaching out as a friend to others. If we recognize this, we can begin to heal wrongs, forgive others' shortcomings, and live more positively.

Job's friends have labored long to pull him out of the mire in which he has put himself. But Job becomes more distant from them, refusing to recognize their help. He probably feels estranged from his friends at a time when they believe they are giving him all that they have within them.

Job's friends believe they are helping him, but Job does not believe what they are saying!

side-tracked by other activities—which are added to the list, of course! But often, making a list of positive, productive "to dos" is the beginning of getting me going for the day—up and at my life in spite of pain.

- What do you know you should be doing, but have been procrastinating over?

- What are three things that you would truly like to accomplish today? This week? This year? What are the small steps you could take toward those goals?

The book of Job could continue for chapter upon chapter, with perhaps even more friends speaking. But with Elihu's speech, the book reflects most of all the salient points of the lesson: Job cannot understand why he is being afflicted, and he mires himself in anger, frustration, weariness, and self-pity; Job's wife tells him to denounce God and die (no comfort there!); Job's three friends try to cajole him out of his sadness and by doing so become frustrated, although they stop at being judgmental; and Elihu castigates Job and his three friends for being so blind and stubborn as to not see the obvious: that it is the lot of humankind to live with pain and there is no reasoning or bargaining with God.

What more could be said?

What more, that is, of a human nature?

Probably not much, at least not until another, more powerful voice delivers the ultimate argument.

In chapter 38, the Lord speaks to Job "out of the storm," and, finally, Job's heart is moved.

Father in heaven,
I ache to hear your voice.
Help me to silence my heart and mind
so that I may truly listen to
your word and your will.
Help me to find perspective in my pain,
and let me rest in comfort
knowing you are with me
at all times.
Amen.

God's Reply

[The Lord addressed Job out of the storm and said]:
"Who is this that obscures divine plans
with words of ignorance?
Gird up your loins now, like a man;
I will question you,
and you tell me the answers!"

JOB 38:1-4

Do you think of yourself as courageous?

You? Yes, you!

You are trying to reach beyond the pain that traps you, holds you back, weighs you down. You yearn for a better life. You ache to know the meaning of your suffering.

Where is your courage?

Anytime we approach a daunting task, there is a certain amount of nervousness or fear within us. This helps give us the energy we need to face tough challenges—for example, of an operation or an appointment with a disability administrator.

We're all human, and it is all right to be nervous and anxious at times. It's also all right to give in to the constraints that pain imposes on us.

It's all right to "hibernate" at times and withdraw from the world around us.

But we are still living and breathing. We still have much to give to others and to the world. We want to laugh and enjoy things, people, life.

And so, we need courage.

In chapter 38 of the book of Job, the Lord immediately challenges Job to "gird up [his] loins," that is, to act like an adult instead of whining like a child. The Lord reminds us that we need to approach pain from an adult perspective.

And one of the biggest hallmarks of being an adult is making responsible decisions.

The Lord asks Job a series of rhetorical questions to which we (and Job) already know the answers.

"Have you comprehended the breadth of the earth?" (Job 38:18)

"Can you raise your voice among the clouds?" (Job 38:34)

"Do you give the horse his strength?" (Job 39:19)

The answer is, of course, no. Human beings can do none of these things, but only the Lord.

All through his suffering, Job has been trying to understand, deny, and throw off his suffering, much like a petulant child tries to avoid unpleasant things. When the Lord presents the breadth of all that he is, Job begins to bend. He begins to grow up.

He begins to see that, for all his desire, he might never fully know the reason why for his pain, nor is it assured that he will ever be cured.

These revelations are particularly poignant today, when we live with the dominance of science and scientific research. Ours is not a world that is comfortable with admitting something is unknowable. Sometimes, for example, when I read about the latest study, I feel as if we're meant to believe that it will only be a few days or weeks and everything from the tiniest molecule to the greatest galaxy will be dissected, categorized, and controlled.

Whenever I see a parent trying to calm a child throwing a tantrum in public, I say a prayer for the parent first, and then the child. Why the parent first? No matter what the circumstance, I always think it must be so hard to know that this child you love is emotionally out of control and disobedient. It must be easy for that parent to want to get angry, but his or her anger must be held in check, another adult trait, and in its place must be patience, along with firmness.

- As God is Our Father, are there times when you throw tantrums with him? How does God react?

- Do you physically feel better during a tantrum? Afterward? Are there more gentle, less physically draining ways you can release your anger and sorrow? Are you willing to learn?

- Do you use tantrums to drive people away?

We also do not live in a world that accepts pain and illness. Instead, a quick review of television, radio, and print advertising implies just the opposite: There's a fix for whatever ails you, and if there isn't, it's because your doctor doesn't want you to get better; he or she merely wants to continue to take your money.

If I sound harsh, it is because after I've lived with lupus almost all of my life, people still ask me if I'm "cured" yet. Almost every week, I get e-mails, or sometimes telephone calls, from strangers who assure me that they have the "cure." They don't believe me when I explain that, no, I'm not cured and in fact there still is no effective treatment for lupus, let alone a cure.

Perhaps you have experienced this, too—the skeptical look from those who ask if you're all better, as if you are doing something intentional to prolong your agony? Aren't you tempted to shout at these people sometimes? To throw a tantrum?

Oh, here we come again—round the corner to where we need to be. We people of faith are called to be adults in our attitudes toward God, ourselves, and one another—and more.

We are called to be courageous.

How, when we are suffering so very much?

God orders Job to "gird [his] loins like a man." He is, in effect, giving Job a first pointer about enduring hardship with maturity and courage. To be able to withstand pain and listen to God, we need to diligently prepare ourselves for the task. Much like fighting a battle, we arm ourselves with knowledge of our condition, the best treatments we can possibly get, behaviors that enable us to strengthen instead of weaken, and spiritual resilience deepened through prayer and faith.

We nurture good relationships with people who are good friends to us and to whom we can be good friends. We reach out to others, offering them our assistance through prayer or even just a kind word, and in so doing spread Christ's light.

What we say makes a huge difference in setting the tone for our conversations with others, God, and ourselves. The more we banish negative words ("cannot," "will not," "impossible," etc.) from our vocabulary and use positive language instead, the more we will have an arsenal of weaponry against internal or external pessimism and prejudice.

It is telling that God orders Job to be "like a man." That is, God doesn't tell Job to get others to make him be a man. This is another crucial lesson about moving beyond pain and into a life of meaning: The responsibility of strengthening for battle and forging ahead into the fray is ours. Others can help us, but we must be willing to take the steps, to climb the mountain.

We must grow up and move on. Then, and only then, will our courage be apparent to us and inspire others.

Courage?

It is in every action we take, from rising in the morning, visiting a friend, keeping a doctor's appointment, or trying to resolve a conflict with someone who "doesn't understand."

It is in the faith that we reflect, through attendance at Mass, joining in with our church communities, and willingly witnessing to God's presence in the world and our lives.

It is in saying "yes" to God each day, although we do not fully understand his purpose for us.

It is in stopping the relentless "why" and taking up the question, "Lord will you show me how?"

St. Paul wrote: "When I was a child, I used to talk as a child, think as a child, reason as a child; when I became a man, I put aside childish things. At present we see indistinctly, as in a mirror, but then face to face. At present I know partially; then I shall know fully, as I am fully known" (1 Corinthians 13:11–12).

- When it comes to handling your pain, are you an adult or a child?

- What are the behaviors and thoughts that you need to put aside?

- How can you be more adult?

Each of us has done at least one courageous thing in our lives. I recall the first time I had to take a trip by plane after I was diagnosed with lupus. I was in severe pain, bald, carrying bags of medications, and completely unsure of whether I would get violently ill in an unfamiliar place. It would have been easy to refuse to travel, but something inside of me prompted me onward, despite my misgivings. The trip went well, and I now believe that the "something inside of me" was really God's voice prompting me to have courage. If I'd never made the trip, I wouldn't have had the courage to make others—God knew what I needed to do, and I resolved to trust him!

- What is the most courageous thing you've ever done? How can you approach the rest of your life with the same degree of courage?

- Who is the most courageous person you know? How can you emulate his or her approach to courage?

O Lord, you are great, indeed.
I ask that you lead me by the hand
as I strive to strengthen myself in faith and courage.
Help me to be an adult, in faith and in life,
so that I may fully realize the potential you have given me
and show others the way to you.
Amen.

Beyond Pain

[Job said to the Lord],
"I have heard of you by word of mouth,
But now my eye has seen you.
Therefore I disown what I have said,
And repent in dust and ashes."

JOB 42:5–6

In each of our lives, there comes a time when we must make a decision that will affect us for the duration of our earthly journey. Either we must decide to accept God's will, whatever that may be, and resolve to make the most of our lives, or we must decide that we will continue to slog through the mire, shedding dignity, friends, and our faith along the way.

This might seem like a stark way to put it; surely there is a middle ground? Can't we grouse for, say, half of the time and praise God the other half?

Can't we wallow in self-pity on weekends and fight the good Christian fight during the weekdays?

Can't we demand from God total relief, a cure, a sudden miracle one night and agree that his will be done the next?

Not really.

Oh, we can in our humanness feel and express anger, frustration, and impatience. But to rest on these would be to sink further in the mire. It is as if we would be telling God we accept this wonderful gift of life only partially, or that we honor him only part time. If we put only half of our effort into being positive and striving to be good witnesses, eventually the other half, the negative half, would overshadow any good we could do. Negativity has a way of casting its shadow far beyond the confines of the moment in which it is expressed or acted on.

If we accept God's will one day, but reject it the next, how can we possibly move forward? Forward, that is, beyond pain?

When Job responds to the Lord at the beginning of chapter 42, he has finally and completely accepted who he is and who God is. He has finally realized that there will be some things he won't understand—but that this is all right. For the Lord is truly great, and Job desires, now, to follow him and not his futile quest for a human answer to a divine situation.

As we have seen with Job, getting to the place of acceptance does not happen overnight, but it is possible if we work through the layers of our pain, frustration, grief, and inability to understand our lives as they are. It is much like peeling back the layers of an onion, and we will shed many tears along the way. But, when we do accept God and put aside our own expectations and egos, when we gird ourselves and resolve to live with courage as adults of faith, then we can move ahead.

- What is standing in your way of accepting your life as it is now?

- What steps can you take next to get closer to acceptance?

Job says something curious as he responds to God in verse 42:5. He speaks of having heard of God before, but now his eyes "have seen" the Lord. But nowhere does it say that God appeared to Job in a vision or the proverbial Moses Moment of a burning bush.

Where, then, did Job see God?

The answer lies in what the Lord says in the previous chapters. The Lord, in truth, is inside, outside, and all around the universe. He can be seen in the roaring of the waves and the beauty of flowers. He can be seen everywhere—even in our lives and hearts.

Job, then, does what we can do, too. He sees God's presence, acknowledges the awesomeness of what the Lord can do and has created. And he fully humbles himself and repents of what he said in his haughtiness before.

In a very real way, Job finally moves beyond his pain. Now, he is able to take positive steps to get back to living.

Job intercedes on behalf of his friends and the Lord pardons them. The Lord restores Job's prosperity, and Job is reconciled with his family and friends. Job becomes a father again, and gives an inheritance to his daughters as well as his sons, something that was highly unusual for his time. He does not rest on his restored vitality, but rather shares it and his spirit with others—the ultimate lesson for us, who crave lives of meaning with and in spite of our pain.

Will it be the same for us, then? If we totally embrace God's will, are we to expect a restoration of wealth, friends, family, and health? Or, is that the point of the lessons of Job? I think that rather than expect material benefits from saying "yes" to the Lord, we can first expect joy.

Joy? Yes, joy.

There is nothing so joyous as, for example, taking our suffering and resolving to live courageously. There is nothing so joyous as reaching out to another in friendship and developing a wonderful, supportive relationship.

Joy springs from Job's ability to surround himself with friends. It also comes from his confession, repentance, and redemption.

Joy in our lives does not have to spring from things, but assuredly springs from our hearts full of gratitude, resolve, and strength.

Job's restoration does not put him exactly where he started. He is older, wiser, and more appreciative of what God has given him. He also strives to bring his friends and family into closer communion with God. He becomes a stronger witness to good than he ever was before, even providing inheritances for his daughters.

When we are deep in the mire, our "before" seems idyllic. But those "good times" pale when we experience the profound joy our lives take on when we fully step into God's light and love. The "after," laced with pain and suffering, takes on more hope than we thought we could have, if we strive each day to accept God's hand and let him lead.

Loving someone has its ups and downs, but the constant is the knowledge that we do love that person.

Loving God can be difficult at times, too, because we are so very human. In our humanness, it is all right to cry, get angry, be frustrated. But in order to stay on a positive course, we understand that those emotions can pass, will pass. Our love for the Lord is not part time, but for always.

Reaching out to others is an excellent way to take Christ's light and shine it into another's darkness. It is also an ideal way to take us out of our suffering and help us move and act beyond pain.

- Who needs your help today?
- What is the most positive lesson from living with pain, and how can you teach it to others?

Job's journey instructs us in how to overcome our human failings and egos and recognize that the Lord's ways might be inscrutable, but his presence in our lives is constant. Through Job's interaction with his friends, we see how important it is to have others we can count on, and we recognize the importance of being polite, willing to help, and having a sense of humor. And, with Job's life "after" his suffering begins, we see that teaching others about the Lord and setting a faith-filled example are but the beginning of nurturing joy within us and in those around us.

As we move from the Old Testament to the New, we move from the "old" world to the "new"—From Job, we go to Jesus and we learn a whole new level of meaning to pain and suffering—and an example to inspire us to the core of our being.

Heavenly Father,
I know that you can do all things.
You made all things.
You made me.
Help me in my humanity
to do with this life you have given me
things that build and do not tear down,
things that give you praise and do not condemn,
things that sow joy and do not make sad.
Praise you, Father!
Amen.

Here are some questions to consider with others or on your own:

1. How is my life similar to Job's "before" pain? Do I think it was better than it really was?

2. Who are my true friends? What have I done for them lately? Do I thank them for being present in my life?

3. How have others reacted to my pain and the limitations it puts on my life?

4. Have I ever used my pain as an excuse to get out of doing something for someone else?

5. What is the best part of my life right now?

6. What is my prayer routine? What can I do to pray more often?

JESUS

Our Light and Hope

[...] but we even boast of our afflictions, knowing that affliction produces endurance, and endurance, proven character, and proven character, hope, and hope does not disappoint, because the love of God has been poured out into our hearts through the holy Spirit that has been given to us. For Christ, while we were still helpless, yet died at the appointed time for the ungodly...God proves his love for us in that while we were still sinners Christ died for us.

ROMANS 5:3—6:8

In the Old Testament, those suffering illness, deformity, and pain are often considered social pariahs, people for whom good fortune and God's approval seem to have been cast aside. The lessons of Job (humility, gratitude, and outreach to others) are valuable to us today. But even more inspirational for us are the lessons imparted to us by Jesus Christ, especially his message of love, respect, and salvation available to all people.

Through his ministry, example, and ultimate sacrifice of death on the cross, Jesus brings those who suffer hope to do more than merely endure their lives—he breathes new energy and life into those who are faltering. His Sermon on the Mount offers food for those whose lives are torn by grief, poverty, despair, and pain. His abiding love embraces all, regardless of their station in life.

Jesus was the Son of God, divine in every way. But he also walked upon the earth and among the people of the day, and in this, he suffered much before his excruciating trek to Calvary. He experienced very human emotions, becoming enraged, weeping, and, one has to imagine, laughing, too. At a time when everybody but the most fortunate normally traveled on foot, our Lord walked roads choked by dust, peppered with stones, abuzz with biting flies, and baked by scorching sun—a far cry from our air-conditioned automobiles and buses.

Jesus was not a wealthy man when he set out on his journey, nor did he acquire wealth along the way. He did not have a steady income, a savings account, health insurance, or government assistance—things that many of us take for granted today.

Yet for all of these discomforting obstacles, our Lord was not deterred from carrying out his mission. Rather, he set forth in his ministry enduring much physical and emotional pain, and did not stop when the pain worsened—even unto death. Jesus shows us by his example that we need not have millions of dollars or be pain-free before doing God's work. Rather, we need to take who we are, all that we are, and set forth, just as he did.

Jesus also reminds us that, if God could send his only Son to die for us, we should understand that our lives will be a mixture of joy and pain. Job learned this. But what is so very different here, and what sheds warm, bright light upon our lives, is that God is not only greater than we are in our suffering, he is also all-loving. Illness is not a punishment, nor is it an indication of moral failings or poor character. From Job's "woe is me…" Jesus brings us to "blessed are we…."

How wonderful is the Lord!

The joy that Job experiences at the end of his story is very much an earthly joy—his prosperity is restored, he feels better, he is accepting of who he is and who God is. Job's joy comes from his trials and his ability to develop strength, courage, and self-awareness.

The joy that Jesus brings is far beyond any that we experience on earth. It is a divine joy that culminates in the reality of the resurrection, the Lord's promise fulfilled. We still need strength, courage, and self-awareness to build our faith and ministry. But we have Jesus' light to guide us, and his example to follow. This is a tall order, especially if we are physically and emotionally frail. But, as we know, nothing is impossible with God...And if we have glimmers of this truth in the Old Testament, in the New Testament we meet the full reality of this truth from the very beginning of Christ's remarkable life.

O Lord,
so very often my pain makes me feel old.
Help me in the coming days and nights
renew my energy and youth of spirit.
Light my life with your grace
and fill me with your hope.
Help my faith overcome
the pain that weighs me down.
Amen.

Humble Beginnings

*"Why were you looking for me? Did you not know
that I must be in my Father's house?"*

LUKE 2:49

Unrelenting pain can, at times, seem like the most horrible thief. It robs us of our health, happiness, energy, mobility, and sometimes our dreams. The longer it ravages our senses, the more it takes center stage and the more we feel depleted.

Perhaps in your terrible pain, you've said things like, "I don't have enough patience to endure this," or, "If I had more money/connections/supportive people/a higher education, I could handle this, but as I am, I'm helpless," or, "It's no use even trying to accomplish anything when I'm in so much pain."

It's not unusual to feel this way; There have been many days when I've barely been able to get out of bed in the morning, let alone take on the rest of the day with any degree of zeal. But even at the very lowest of times, I've learned to understand that resting, sleeping, "just being with the pain" are all necessary parts of the whole cloth of the life God has given me. I'm not doing "nothing" when I rest, for example; I'm helping my body relax and recharge. Also, whether I feel a lack of internal or external resources does not trouble me so very much if I am keeping God central in prayer, thought, and faith.

When we look at the most painful, need-filled moments of our lives as meaningful and value-full, we can begin to appreciate them more, even when we are laid low and lowly. Lifting existence from the merely physical toward the divine is a God-given ability that pain and, indeed, society, do not encourage, but that we have the calling and the understanding to achieve.

We have the example of our Lord to thank for this.

Unlike Job, whose life was at its zenith when trouble struck him, Jesus' life began humbly and painfully. At no time during his earthly journey did our Lord enjoy abundant material wealth, nor did he command everyone's respect; throughout his ministry, Christ was subject to derision from those in power and those not. As miraculous as his birth was, the first visitors he received—shepherds—were considered outcasts in society, and his first bed was a manger.

In our society's language today, Jesus would probably be considered "at risk": born in a lowly place and station and looking forward to a life of hard work with little material comfort. Not a lot is expected of

We have no control over the situation into which we are born. Yet, God lovingly knows each of us by name and has a very special life to give each of us. It is so important that we remember that this wonderful gift—life—is greater than any of the material possessions we might have or could have had. With our lives, we can bring God's word and love to others. We can help others in distress. We can encourage others. We can inspire people born into lowly circumstances, and it was probably assumed by those outside the Holy Family that Jesus' life would follow a trajectory like that of a typical manual laborer, leaving little lasting impact besides the children he would raise.

But Mary and Joseph knew, as did Jesus, that the baby born into near-poverty would shake and shape the world. The baby in Bethlehem was born with a distinct, divine identity and purpose, and the environment of his upbringing provided fertile ground on which for him to advance "in wisdom and age and favor before God and man" (Luke 2:52).

We see in Jesus' early life that very little can yield very great things.

So it is, too, with us who live with excruciating pain.

Yes, it is tempting to think that we cannot do anything with our lives unless we have a lot of money or unless people in high places lift us up. Medications cost a lot of money sometimes, and getting in to see the best specialists can take months, if we can find the right doctor to refer us.

If we are mobility-impaired, it is also easy to think that there are activities that are off-limits to us, and places that are closed.

others. Our lives, our precious lives, are amazing, unique treasures beyond rubies!

- How often have you said, "Well of course [she/he] can do that; [she/he] has enough money"?

- How do you value the things in your life? Do you think you never have enough things?

- How can you show that you value your life, the most precious gift God has given you to use on this earth?

Pain and complications that stem from it can cause us to lose our jobs, which are major determinants of our socials identity. The resulting economic hit, as well as the loss of a sense of productivity, belonging, and being of use, can take us further downward.

We might think we are nowhere near as strong and savvy as we need to be to advocate for ourselves in medical and personal situations.

But we can reach beyond the expectations of society and our own limitations. We are children beloved of God; each of us has a distinct purpose and is called by name to fulfill that purpose. What's more, from strong faith, prayer and determination can grow a sense of discernment that will lead each of us along the path God has laid out for us. And the Lord walks with us each step.

After his lowly birth, Jesus lived with Mary and Joseph as any child lives with his parents. He probably started to learn Joseph's trade as a carpenter as soon as he was old enough to do so—in Mary and Joseph's world, few people, young or old, sat around doing nothing! Joseph and Mary probably taught him about the Jewish faith through Sabbath and other rituals and storytelling. Certainly, Jesus did not attend a private prep school and take advanced placement courses!

And yet, when he was twelve and went with his parents to the Temple in Jerusalem, he separated himself from them and sat with the elders, asking questions and speaking in such a learned way that all who heard were astounded.

This first glimpse into Jesus' mind and heart is a beautiful way to convey a lesson to us pain sufferers today—lack of formal education does not mean we are less worthy of good care, consideration, and meaning. We were each of us born with a mind, and it didn't come with a certificate that said, "Good only when the following courses and degree programs have been completed."

Asking questions of someone in authority (a doctor, pharmacist, or insurance administrator, for example) can be a scary proposition. Next time you need to get answers, try using the tools a journalist uses when researching a story:

- Who? (Who do I need to talk to? Seek a second opinion from?)

- What? (What is my diagnosis? What tests or medications are needed? What can I do today that is positive and life-affirming?

- When? (When can I expect to see improvement from my treatment? When will my test results be available?)

- Where? (Where should I write my letter of appeal for my latest insurance claim?)

- Why? (Why is it necessary for me to take the medication you prescribe?)

- How? (How can I become more involved in my health care situation? How can I be a better role model to others?

Of course, how we develop our minds is important, and that we continue to grow and learn is vital to our well-being (and brain function). In the Temple in Jerusalem, Jesus asked many questions, demonstrating a need to learn from others. We, too, should ask questions of our doctors, care providers, and anyone from whom we wish to learn.

Jesus also posed questions to learned elders in the Temple—he went to the "experts" in the subject in which he was seeking answers. This is something we can keep in mind when we're seeking answers, too. Do we ask our rheumatologist about a tooth problem? A dentist about our arthritis? A random e-mailer who claims to have a "cure" for our troubles about where we can sign up?

So, when we seek answers from God about our purpose in life, to whom do we turn?

One of the greatest gifts we have is the 24/7, 365-days-a-year open line to the Lord. Through prayer, we can learn so very much, especially about our unique gifts and the ministry God intends for each of us. Our questions can find answers if we are attentive, patient, and willing to listen.

As Catholics, we are brought up in the church through religious education punctuated by receiving the sacraments. But after the sacrament of confirmation, our education often comes to an abrupt halt. As with any other subject or skill, our faith grows best when nurtured and challenged by new information, people, and perspectives. We are at our best when we're always learning!

- Do you ever yearn to delve deeper into the faith, perhaps studying Scripture or church history?

- Do you try new ways to pray, or new guides to prayer and Bible study that can help you approach God from a fresh perspective?

I try to spend lots of dedicated time with God in prayer, whether in church or as I go about my day. "Taking Christ with me" is one of my favorite expressions; I can imagine him sitting beside me in my car, standing in line with me at the checkout counter. When I think of Jesus as my constant companion, not only am I never alone, but I feel more empowered to look at the world through fresh, Christian eyes. Truly it makes a difference.

Here's an exercise I like to introduce at my workshops (it's great for getting people moving after sitting still, listening to me talk!). I ask everyone to stand up and start to walk around the room. Just walk. This sometimes takes encouragement—don't we all like to have a purpose or destination when we walk?

After a few moments of "just walking," I tell everyone to stop. Then, I ask them to walk again, but this time imagine Christ walking with each person in the room.

The difference in how people walk, as well as the atmosphere in the room, is noticeable.

Take Jesus along always! He changes everything!

Other ways to learn and grow are all around us. At church, during Mass and other events and services, there are countless ways to reflect, pray, hear Scripture proclaimed and taught. We can learn from one another in fellowship. We can learn from total strangers, as we know that Christ works through each of us.

Learning anything takes attention. It is a very active process. If we keep our eyes, ears and hearts open to what we can learn from God, we will be building our faith and carrying out his plan!

An 85-year-old woman receiving her bachelor's degree.
A 107-year-old celebrating a birthday. A 12-year-old
writing a book and getting it published.

Each day, age holds some people back and it propels
others forward. Whether young or old, those who can
accomplish significant things continue onward toward
their goals because they are driven, not repelled, by
their numerical age. They don't say, "I'm too old to…" or
"I'm too young to…" Do you?

Our Lord surprised everyone when he asked questions in the
Temple. Not only did people think he came from such a lowly back-
ground that he couldn't possibly be that educated, but his speech be-
lied his age. He was so young, too young, they were probably thinking
and whispering amongst themselves.

Yes, Jesus was young. But, as he told his parents, he had to be in
his Father's house. He knew what his mission was, and he was deter-
mined to fulfill it no matter his age or station in life.

You might be years older than Jesus was. Perhaps pain has made
you feel much older still. If so, you might be even less likely to start
something new or try to venture out of your comfort zone because
you feel and think you're "too old."

But what does "too old" mean, exactly? Is there anyone barring the
door to a library, church, or community college classroom, intent on
excluding anyone "of a certain age?"

I'm an avid tennis watcher and weekly player (yes, even though my
knees feel it afterward). There are leagues that are divided into age
groups, including one for eighty- to eight-five-year-olds and upward!
And some of them hit a mean backhand slice!

Whatever God intends for each of us, I'm certain that he doesn't look at us in terms of how many years, months, and days we've walked on this earth. Rather, he considers us by what's in our hearts, what we've done with our talents and gifts, and how we've treated ourselves and others. Who we are is far more important than how old we are.

As you think about moving beyond your pain and following God's personal call for you, consider how you view your age. If it seems to be an impediment (the "I'm too old" kind), consider this: Time passes anyway. Next year, you'll be older than you are now. Do you want to be on your way, or stalled? Moving ahead, or treading water?

When we think in terms of how quickly time passes, we can better understand that even small steps move us into productive, prayer-filled, joyous lives.

What doesn't matter is our age.

In many ways, it is easier to identify with Jesus' humble beginnings. It's where most of us started out. We can appreciate his eagerness to get started on his mission. We felt that same impatience waiting for high school graduation or some other goal. We can also identify with the constraints put upon our Lord at the time. He was only twelve, and he had to go home with his parents. That must have been hard for him in a way, being back home to Nazareth, learning carpentry. He had undergone his experience in Jerusalem, and no doubt looked forward to the day when he could set forth once again.

For you, maybe, life "before pain" is something you look back/forward to. That is, you had a taste of what life was going to be like, and you couldn't wait until it got started.

As you are now, in pain and suffering, it is important to keep in mind the things you want to do and feel you are called to do. But remember Job? When he finally went back home, after his trials, he was a changed man. He saw things differently and behaved differently. Sometimes, our outlook and circumstances change, too.

As we move forward with our pain, we have many expectations. How we learn to manage them and deal with the unexpected is vital to becoming even stronger—and even more secure in our Christ-led walk.

We don't learn much about the rest of Jesus' childhood in the gospels. By the time he sets about his ministry, he is thirty years old and well past precocious childhood. I often wonder what he thought, setting out from home, knowing what his life would be for the next three years. Did he know he couldn't expect the same awe as the elders in the Temple had for him when he was twelve?

Change. Challenge. Great peril and pain.

How did Jesus face these as he set forth on his ministry?

Jesus,
help me cultivate my humility as a way
to better shine your light of truth and love.
In prayer, help me listen.
In learning, help me persevere.
In how I value things, help me moderate.
And in how I live my life, help me be ever mindful
that this life is precious
in every way.
Amen.

Going Forth

"This is my beloved Son, with whom I am well pleased!

MATTHEW 3:17

Before we can run the proverbial marathon, we have to take our first small steps. We have to put on the proper shoes. Trot around the block a few times. We learn to deal with pain and the temptation to stop training when we feel too sore and discouraged to continue.

In his wisdom, Jesus knew this completely and demonstrated it in how he set forth on his three-year journey from Nazareth to Calvary. He did not leave his familial home and immediately begin preaching to large crowds. Rather, he "put on the proper shoes" first.

He sought out John the Baptist, his cousin who was preaching of the coming of the Messiah and baptizing people in the Jordan River. Jesus wanted to be baptized, too, a sign of living faith with which he would christen, so to speak, his ministry.

John the Baptist was surely an eyeful! Dressed in camel's hair clothing and a leather belt, and living on a diet of locusts and wild honey, the man was hardly mainstream. But he recognized Jesus immediately, hesitating to baptize Jesus because he knew who he really was.

One of the things that can make people hesitate about venturing forth from a "comfort zone" is the fear of being ostracized, or, in the case of people with visible disabilities, the fear of being stared at or ridiculed. We lupus patients, for example, have to avoid sun exposure even on the hottest of days, so when everyone else is in shorts, tank tops and flip-flops, we're dressed in long-sleeved shirts, long pants, and wide-brimmed hats. Oh, we get the stares!

I have known brilliant people with significant mobility issues, due in some cases to cerebral palsy or the after-effects of polio. I've seen able-bodied adults dismiss them—for example, not addressing them directly for their order at a restaurant because they assume they're incapable of speaking for themselves.

Being alone and being obvious can be very scary.

But being with like-minded and like-bodied people can give a feeling of protection and camaraderie that brings courage and self-esteem. And it also helps the sufferer better understand the things he or she needs to do to be active in the world at large.

If you hesitate to go out to a restaurant, movie, or other venue because you're afraid of what might happen, consider asking a friend who also deals with physical issues to accompany you. Compare notes on how you both deal with adverse situations, and bring the gifts of laughter and strength along, too!

John the Baptist might have looked like an outcast, but he was essential to Jesus' journey. By insisting that John baptize him, Jesus reminds us of his own humanity and communion with us. Each time I witness a baptism or think of my own, I remember that our Lord, too, was baptized. An awesome commonality!

So, Jesus was baptized. And the Spirit of God descended like a dove, and a voice from the heavens said, "This is my beloved Son, with whom I am well pleased" (Matthew 3:17).

With such a definitive validation of Jesus' identity, surely everyone would accept him and embrace his message. Surely he would begin converting throngs of people.

We might expect so, but Jesus did not.

Instead of moving forward to his preaching, Jesus did an unexpected thing: He distanced himself from all others, went into the desert, and fasted for forty days and forty nights. There, in that time, he was tempted by the Devil.

Have you ever made plans to finally get to do something you've always wanted to do…and it turns out completely different from the way you planned?

Taking the first baby steps out of our comfort zone can be frightening, exciting, and uplifting all at the same time. We have such great expectations! We've prepared our bodies for the event, made plans for how our day will go. We've mustered up all of our inner strength to overcome the obstacles that have stood in our way. And, suddenly, as soon as we leave the safety of our life inside our cocoon, we come face to face with challenge, temptation, and hardship.

What, you might ask, is the point of even trying to go beyond my world of pain if I can't even plan a pleasant outing without things turning out so very wrong?

Jesus' experience in the desert is, on the face of it, an unpleasant one. But if we look at it more deeply, we see that, once again, our Lord demonstrates ways to combat the human characteristics that threaten to keep us from fully living our Christ-centered ministries.

Jesus had just come from being baptized and the very overt validation of God declaring him "beloved Son." A merely human reaction to this would be to feel egotistical, to "ride high" on the crest of such a singular pronouncement. Instead, Jesus went into the desert, a physical wasteland, a way of bringing humility to his humanity.

Even in the desert, Satan tried to appeal to Jesus' ego. "The tempter" tried to get Jesus to turn stones into loaves of bread and cause angels to lift him up.

How did Jesus handle these temptations, these plays on his human ego?

He responded to the temptations with firm refusals and verbal ammunition provided by Scripture: "You shall not put the Lord, your God, to the test" (Matthew 4:7).

Living with pain may seem like living in a desert. Perhaps you get to such a dry, forbidding place with your suffering that any balm sounds enticing. You want relief—any relief—and you find yourself turning to temptations like anger, alcohol, more drugs, or advertised "cures" at an ever-increasing rate.

- Have you considered that you are experiencing that same kind of temptation that our Lord did at times like these?

- How can you handle temptations in a more Christ-like manner?

Now, as our Lord was repelling Satan, he was also experiencing physical deprivation and, probably, ever-increasing pain. He had fasted for forty days and nights in the desert. He must have felt physically very weak. But his reaction to Satan shows us that the spirit can still be strong in the face of physical stresses. And, it shows us something more: When we might be too weak to think of the words, we can rely on God to help us.

Jesus, of course, knew exactly what to say to Satan. But he also relied upon Scripture verses to punctuate his intent. The more we read and study and learn from Scripture, the better equipped we will be to do the same thing—to rely on the inspired words of Scripture to guide us and communicate for us at times when we are being tried.

One way that I try to bring this element of the Lord into my life is when I am particularly confused or at sea about something. The first example of this in my life with lupus came before I was definitively diagnosed.

My hair had been falling out in cylindrical clumps for almost a year. I also had other symptoms, but not knowing what lupus was, let alone what its symptoms were, I couldn't even articulate that these, too, were problems. My doctors had all said that I was "just stressed." That was it.

During one appointment with my dermatologist, I prayed that the Lord would guide my words. I suspected something terrible was wrong with me, but didn't know what it was. The next words that came out of my mouth seemed as if from someone else.

"Can't you please take some blood tests to see what else is going wrong?" I asked the doctor.

She said, "Oh, I'm sure that's not necessary. You're just stressed."

I prayed again, asking God for more guidance and strength. It came!

"Please humor me. It's my blood, my money, my time. If nothing else is wrong, then at least I'll know," I said.

She finally agreed. A month later, abnormal blood tests in hand, I was diagnosed by a rheumatologist and began treatment.

So often we think we should know what to say or do in critical situations, but we really don't. The Lord, however, can guide our hearts, minds, and tongues and give us just the right words to say—if we ask him in faithful prayer. No matter how much in pain we are, no matter how great our confusion or fear, God inspires!

> Because pain can make us feel like victims of our condition, it is natural to feel helpless, too. At times like those, we can pray for guidance and also remember Christ's strength in the desert and the way he stood up to Satan and his temptations. We can also practice our responses to temptations before they taunt us, and strengthen our resolve in this manner, too.

After the desert, Jesus still did not immediately embark on his ministerial journey. His cousin, John the Baptist, was arrested, and Jesus left the area, moving on to Galilee. It probably would have been dangerous for Jesus to stay in Nazareth because of his ties to John the Baptist. But it must have been bittersweet to leave the area and the fate of his cousin unknown—an emotional setback for him personally and for his ministry.

In our lives, we will experience setbacks, too. Sometimes, we are all set to embark on a new activity or develop a new relationship when our health takes a downturn and we have to put the plans on hold. Or, we experience a loss, as Jesus did, with the death of a loved one (John the Baptist was executed), a move (Jesus had to leave Nazareth), or other change.

"Life happens," is a phrase I employ in these cases. And, it is not easy, especially as setbacks and unhappy events can cause terrible stress and upheaval.

Still, we cannot control much of what happens around us. And the losses in life are all part of being human. What does matter is how we deal with the losses, how we allow ourselves to mourn and move on, to sorrow and to strengthen.

"Good" or "bad" stress is still stress and can upset the most carefully laid plans. In an ideal world, we would be able to handle stress with grace, but we humans are somewhat less than ideal! So it's essential to develop and practice techniques to handle stress and setbacks. Some of these include:

- Controlled deep breathing, stretching and other physical activity to relax tensed muscles

- Prayer and meditation to promote spiritual calm and greater closeness with the support and love of God

- Calling upon loved ones for encouragement and help in times of great stress and upheaval

- Learning about the stages of grief and other life events to better understand how you react to these traumas and how you can help yourself (and allow others to help you) through them

Another aspect of handling setbacks is how we react to the emotions and actions of others. So often we wish someone would feel differently than they do, or behave in a way other than the one they choose. I hear frequently from patients who lament that their spouse/sibling/parent does not understand their pain. But dwelling on "what is not"—much like dwelling on "before pain"—can add stress upon stress to already overwhelming physical challenges.

The truth is that we cannot control the emotions and actions of another person. As with conversion to faith, conversion to a more enlightened ability to cope with another's suffering has to come from within a person; no amount of nagging from someone else will change a heart that is already stony.

When I was first diagnosed with lupus, several of my friends immediately rallied to my aid. Others, however, did not. They eventually stopped calling and issuing invitations to me. Or, if we did talk, they pointedly avoided the subject of my illness and did not even ask me how I was feeling. Their rejection hurt me at first. But eventually I realized that some people simply cannot cope with the idea of illness, let alone the reality. These people might otherwise be good people, but their sense of life's challenges is still immature.

With the rejection from certain people have come acceptance, friendship, and fellowship with others. I rejoice in these God-given relationships, and I pray daily for the people who still struggle with others' suffering, that they will become softened and enlightened.

I've learned that I cannot change the way others react to me, but I can undertake to control the kind of people I surround myself with and the amount of time that I expend to reach out to others who are not so close. The break-up of a relationship, especially one of long

A large part of moving forward from a life focused on pain is being able to forgive others and oneself for perceived or real hurts. It is easy to say, "I forgive," but to take it to heart is something much more difficult. To start the forgiveness process, it is helpful to take a personal inventory and acknowledge any fault you might have had in the hurt inflicted. Ask God for guidance on how to arrive at peace with the person who you feel has wronged you. Pray for acceptance of yourself, and the ability to treasure your gift of life and the love God standing, can be devastating. But we must trust that God will guide us to nurturing relationships and help us forgive those who are hurtful.

From the time he sat in the Temple in Jerusalem at age twelve and questioned the elders there, Jesus demonstrated the need to reach out to others and involve them in his ministry. It is no surprise, then, that after he left Nazareth, he sought out disciples. The first two he chose were Simon (Peter) and his brother Andrew, fishermen in the Sea of Galilee. Two others, James and John, joined them soon after, and Jesus began preaching, drawing large crowds, and "curing every disease and illness among the people" (Matthew 4:23).

With his ministry under full sail, Jesus had more than enough work to do—a far cry from his earlier life, tucked away in Nazareth! During the next days and weeks, added to physical discomfort would be challenges to our Lord's energy and time, as well as emotional setbacks that brought stresses of their own.

We pain sufferers can learn much from not only what our Lord said during the short years of his ministry, but also from how he handled the ever-growing list of challenges that assailed him each day.

pours out for you. Take the process of forgiveness step-by-step, day-by-day. If the person you want to forgive refuses you and your attempts to make peace, still work on peace within yourself and let it settle into your soul and refresh you.

- Whom do I want to forgive?
- What steps can I take today to bring me closer to peace of mind and closer to God?
- Do I understand that I cannot control the emotions and actions of others toward me and my suffering?

O Lord,
in the days and weeks ahead,
help me to better discern how
to cope with setbacks.
Give me the courage to face change
with open eyes and willing hands.
And enable me to choose wisely
those things and people
that bring you glory and honor.
Amen.

Working Wonders

[Jesus said]: "Is a lamp brought in
to be placed under a bushel basket or under a bed,
and not to be placed on a lampstand?"

MARK 4:21

In the desert heat, with simple food, rocky roads and the beginnings of harsh criticism, Jesus and his disciples traveled, preached and
ministered to the growing numbers of followers who recognized his
divine ministry. Word of Jesus' miracles spread; his reputation as a
healer became known throughout Galilee and beyond. More disciples
joined him. And the crowds grew larger still.

Today, we marvel at the stories of Jesus' many healings. And, as
people who suffer from illness and pain, often we yearn to be healed
ourselves.

Why is it that some devout people live in unending pain while others are cured?

This is the very question Job asked, long before Jesus walked on
earth. It is the question Job finally realized he could not answer; only
God really knows the reason.

Moving forward with all of the challenges of pain requires tremendous dedication and faith. It also requires stamina. Jesus must have been in excellent physical shape to be able to travel on foot each day and devote his attention to preaching and healing! The apostles recognized the athletic nature of ministry, too. In 2 Timothy 4:7, St. Paul says, "I have competed well; I have finished the race; I have kept the faith."

The more we take care of our bodies and strengthen them through healthful habits, the more effective we will be in our families, communities, and lives.

- What unhealthful habits do I need to change?

- What can I do to enable my body to strengthen and be better prepared for my life's journey?

But it is helpful to make a distinction between the words "heal" and "cure." Often, they are used interchangeably. In the context of faith and wellness and suffering, however, they have different nuances of meaning.

"To cure" means, essentially, that all signs and symptoms of an illness or adverse health condition are eradicated, gone for good. "To heal" also means "to cure," but within a spiritual context, it also means to "make whole," that is, "to bring closer to or be in closer communion with God."

When we understand these two distinctive meanings for "to heal," we can also conclude that, although not everyone will be "cured" of their illness in this life, each person can certainly be "healed," that is, brought closer to God and peace of spirit, even along with suffering.

In fact, it is this meaning of "to heal" that resonates most with me as I live through each day with my multiple serious, chronic illnesses. I know that God wants me to be healed, to be closer to him, even if he chooses not to cure me. It is this sense of healing and closeness to our Lord that breathes energy and inspiration into me each day.

I can live without being cured. I would be nothing without God's healing.

Reflect on the two meanings of "cure" and "heal." Focus on thinking in terms of being healed, that is, getting closer to God, and allow his peace to grow ever stronger.

- How likely is it that I will be cured of my illness? If unlikely, how do I feel about this?

- How can I move past my anger and frustration to renew my resolve to live a life of meaning even with my suffering?

As our Lord's work increased, so did the demands on his time. Not long after he began his Galilean ministry, people pursued him day and night (Mark 1:32). At such times, Jesus did something that is a good lesson for us, too.

He took time to be alone in prayer and to rest.

You might wonder why, in a book about going "beyond" pain, I will speak of the importance of taking time to be alone and to rest. Aren't we called to be actively engaged in ministry to others and the world around us?

Yes, we are. But as we see in Jesus' life, there is a very important place in our schedules for reflective, restful time. If we don't take this time to recharge, we will undoubtedly run out of steam, physically, emotionally, and spiritually. We might make ourselves sicker, more pained, than we were previously. We might become discouraged and give up at a time when God is most calling us to act.

Jesus not only knew this, he practiced this. He set the example for us—and a wise example it is!

I know, for instance, that on the days when my pain is less and I'm feeling more energetic, I tend to do too much. "Get while the getting's good" is a Midwestern phrase that I've used on more than one occasion.

How do I feel the next day, after I've packed every possible moment with activity?

Exhausted. Spent. Possibly worse than my previous "bad" day.

Jesus never made an excuse for his taking time to pray and rest. He did not apologize to his followers when he needed to get away. He simply did what he had to do.

We, however, might be overcome with guilt at taking time for ourselves, genuine rest time that helps us relax and get necessary energy back to continue on. (Notice I say, "genuine"; there's a huge difference between sloth and taking time to rest!) Praying for guidance and comfort can help assuage feelings of guilt, as can understanding that rest is medicine as powerful and necessary as some of the pills and other treatments our doctors prescribe for us. Another helpful way to approach rest is to schedule it on a calendar, as you would a doctor's appointment, and keep to the schedule.

As people who live with physical challenges, we have to learn to balance activity with enough rest in order to be as fully functioning as possible on the "good" days. We also have to do this so that we don't do ourselves any harm. To do so would be to create a very vicious cycle of hectic activity, horrible pain, frustration, more pain, and even more frustration.

The mire in which Job was stuck can trap us, too, when we try to do too much. The rest that comes with prayer is also vital for us to keep our spirits centered on God's way and wisdom. We need that peaceful time of communication with the Lord in order to refresh our spirits

In a life of pain, we often feel as if there is little under our control. However, in many ways we have complete control over how we spend our time, whether we waste precious moments or make full use of even the short spans we are capable of offering to others. When we consider how much we can take on at one time, it is very important to understand that "no" is not a swear word! In fact, it is often advisable to use it frequently, especially at times when health is particularly fragile.

Saying "no" gives us the breathing room to be able to say "yes" at a better time. And it helps us maintain control over our schedules, which in turn helps us manage our health and energy better.

- Is there anything I did today that I could have put off until tomorrow, or a better time?

- How can I become more comfortable with saying "no" when I know that saying "yes" will bring me more pain and trouble than I should have?

and strengthen our direction for the days ahead. Each day's prayer "retreat" is a time to close out distractions and things that take from us and build up resilience and grace inside so that it can shine forth, like the lamp that Jesus speaks of in the Gospel of Mark.

Taking time for rest and prayer gave Jesus the ability to intensify his ministry, not lessen it. He used his time wisely, understanding that his days on earth were finite and his work ever greater. And he was able to keep his focus, even when interrupted by visits from his family (Mark 3:31–35) and his disciples' fear of a sudden, violent storm (Mark 4:35–41).

Time management is something that each of us struggles with. With an unpredictable health condition, it can seem as if time is completely out of our control. (Again, that awesome word, "control!") Here are some suggestions for more effective time management:

- Understand when you are most functional during the day and plan activities accordingly.

- Understand when you have the least amount of energy during the day and, if at all possible, schedule nothing or very simple tasks during that time.

- Break down tasks into smaller time increments and accomplish these one at a time, even over a period of days.

- Keep a log of how you spend your time each day for a week. At the end of a week, review your time spent and be honest about where you wasted time. Resolve to do better the next week.

In Mark, chapters 1–5, Jesus not only works miracles, he also relates a number of parables. One that can resonate with pain sufferers is the parable of the mustard seed.

From his own humble beginnings, Jesus himself embodies the parable of something great coming from something small. His influence reached far beyond the borders of Nazareth, and his ministry touched (and still touches) more lives than we can possibly count. For us, too, we might never know when or how a word or deed from us might positively impact another's life.

I had just such an experience last year. I was walking through my neighborhood on a chilly, overcast day, and I happened to pass by a home I'd seen many times before. My neighborhood is full of apartment buildings, but there are one or two stalwart single-family homes in the mix. This one in particular was one of my favorites because whoever lived there had taken great pains to nurture an amazing garden. Lush trees, brilliant flowers, vegetables year-round—the garden was an oasis in urban surroundings.

On this particular day, the gentleman who owned the house was working in his garden. I was really excited to meet him. I stopped and introduced myself and then told him I was so grateful for the work he did in his garden. It was a pleasure to walk by and see it—a real gift to the neighborhood.

His face took on a peculiar look, almost as if he couldn't decide whether he was going to smile or weep. After a few moments of silence, he said, "I appreciate your saying that. Just before you came up to me, I'd decided to just sell the place and let them tear it down and build condos. After what you said, I think I'm going to keep the house and the garden as is."

I was stunned. I asked him why he'd want to sell. He said, "There's a woman in the neighborhood. Every time my flowers are in bloom, she comes over and picks them. Takes them for herself. Just cuts them down. Today, I saw her and told her to stop. She yelled at me that my garden was for everyone to just take what they wanted. So, I thought, I'm not going to do this anymore."

Now, I really thought he was going to cry. But when he spoke, his voice was calm. "But what you just said to me makes me want to keep going. Thank you."

We talked a little more, and then I went back to my walk and he to his garden.

The whole incident really brought home to me that even the smallest of seeds, a simple "thank you," for example, can be a powerful way to bring light and hope. Our caring, however small, can grow into a mustard plant of strength.

Jesus became so popular that he couldn't hide from the crowds that followed him. As quickly as his renown grew, so did criticism from the elders and scribes who disapproved of his actions and timing. By chapter 3 of the Gospel of Mark, people were already plotting to kill him (Mark 3:6). Yet our Lord had a remarkable ability to focus on his ministry and on doing great works in spite of the turmoil brewing about him.

In this, I feel we have a vital piece of the puzzle of how to keep going, to reach beyond our suffering, to nurture lives of meaning: The more we cultivate God's peace and presence within us, the more focused we will be on doing his work.

It is no happenstance that Jesus speaks of the lampstand in the Scripture verse from the Gospel of Mark that starts off this chapter. A light brings brightness and also warmth. It illuminates fear and extinguishes it with reality, then tempers that reality with comfort and grace. But a light does not burn in a vacuum, nor can it illuminate darkness if it is hidden away.

Truly, God's peace sheds light in the darkest corners of our souls, and when we reflect that light upon others, we are doing God's work. And what an awesome thing it is to know that we, with pain and illnesses, are called to work for God!

So, with renewed attention to managing our time and energy, we can let our light shine more brightly. We who suffer don't have as many optimal minutes in a day as others who can make use of all of them.

But, if we take a close look at how we spend our time, we can carve out five, fifteen, sixty more minutes during which we can reach out to others, increase our knowledge of Scripture, be of use in the world.

Be light!

O Lord,
please give me the wisdom
to know how to plant seeds of hope and comfort.
Help me be strong and appreciative
of the time you give me
so that I may make the most of it,
in activity or in rest.
Amen.

Clouds Gather

[Jesus said]: "Take courage, it is I, do not be afraid."

MARK 6:50

Jesus' ministry took him along dusty roads and fly-infested towns. His winding way led him full circle, to his hometown of Nazareth. We might expect that he would be hailed as a kind of hero by the people among whom he had grown up. But that was not what happened.

In the synagogue, where Jesus began to teach, the people who heard him simply could not believe that "the carpenter, the son of Mary" (Mark 6:3) could be so wise and gifted. As he spoke, they became more incensed ("They took offense at him" [Mark 6:3].).

Not exactly a hero's homecoming!

For many reasons, people we know might not believe we are as sick or in as much pain as we say we are. One of the biggest reasons for this is probably that many of us have illnesses and pain that are invisible; we might look perfectly healthy on the outside, while inside we suffer. I suppose it is understandable for people to be skeptical if they don't see or feel what we do. But all too often, their unkind remarks and outright rejection can hurt us deeply.

More than once, I've received e-mails from people facing hurtful skepticism, such as when family members don't believe a person is truly ill, or coworkers say someone felled by pain "just doesn't want to work that hard." I wish the unbelievers could hear what I hear—the sadness, frustration, and hurt they cause.

But I also wish that the sufferers could go from feeling victimized to feeling empowered to educate. So often, ignorance can be countered by someone willing to teach the truth.

Jesus understood this, and his example in the face of hometown rejection gives us another lesson in coping with our own, similar challenges.

> Rejection can be very painful, especially if we encounter it in someone we know. Rejection is also a part of being human, and a very real part of walking with Christ. We do best when we understand this and focus on our walk, modeling our behavior after our Savior.
>
> - How do I handle rejection by others? How could I handle it better?
> - When do I reject others who suffer? How could I better model Christ's behavior toward others?

First, Jesus acknowledged the rejection: "A prophet is not without honor except in his native place and among his own kin and in his own house" (Mark 6:5). He did not doubt his own identity in the process, but merely called others' rejection of him exactly what it was.

Second, Jesus continued to minister, but in the "villages in the vicinity" (Mark 6:6). In other words, he persisted in working in a place where the hometown "crowd" was sure to witness his ministry, but he didn't remain in the central place where those rejecting him congregated—the synagogue in Nazareth. He allowed his example to instruct, and did not make himself available for constant criticism while he carried out his mission.

Third, Jesus sent his disciples out to minister with specific instructions about how they were to handle rejection: "Whatever place does not welcome you or listen to you, leave there and shake the dust off your feet in testimony against them" (Mark 6:11).

These words are very strong and might seem to contradict other things that Christ said, such as "love one another," and "turn the other cheek." Yet, here Jesus is teaching us a very important lesson: Many are in need of ministry and many need to hear God's Word. If the

Jesus did not advocate that we be doormats for those who reject us or our ministry. How, then, do we manage our relationships, and how do we curtail one that is toxic but so woven into our own life that it will be difficult to break it off?

There is no easy answer; every situation is unique. Prayer, guidance from clergy and other Christians, and support from others who suffer are all very useful, especially in the early stages of discerning what relationships are toxic and need to be stopped. Sometimes, managing time better so the contact you have with a toxic individual is minimal is also an option to pursue.

- Are there toxic people in my life?

- How can I focus my actions and time so that I reach out to those who most need me and are open to God's word?

messenger lingers with those who reject him or her, to the point of derision and abuse, then those in need are deprived of ministry.

In our lives, I think this lesson also applies to toxic relationships that drag us down, sap our energy, and work to take us further away from peace of spirit and heart. We've all known people like this—people who seem to take all the life out of a room and who make every excuse not to do what is healthful or helpful to others. Perhaps someone close to you is like this. Perhaps you are married to a person like this.

In instructions to his disciples, Jesus is very clear about where our focus needs to be. We should not allow ourselves to be dragged down by anyone, and we should not allow anyone to keep us from carrying out our own ministry.

The focus of our lives should be to bring light and love into the world, not to succumb to darkness.

Along with rejection came great loss. John the Baptist, who had been imprisoned by Herod, was executed. Herod heard of Jesus' fame and thought that John had been raised from the dead (Mark 6:14), further solidifying the threat that began to gather like a mighty storm cloud over Jesus' ministry.

But Jesus was not daunted. Instead, his miracles took on an even greater magnitude. He fed 5,000 with five loaves and two fish. He walked on water and calmed a storm. He healed many and drew larger crowds than ever before.

Jesus was deeply involved in his ministry. We can feel the force of his focus leap off the pages of Mark's gospel. In these pages, we know so much about our Lord's way of ministering—walking from village to village with barely any possessions. Resting when he could. Empowering others to work wonders, too.

These pages are all about Jesus' work and not much, if anything, about Jesus himself.

Of course, Jesus' ministry was inextricably identifiable with him, the Son of God. But it was amazingly devoid of something we often have trouble hiding: ego.

About once a week, I hear from someone—a friend of a friend, or a total stranger—who has been living with illness and pain and wants to write a book about it. The first question I always ask is, "What do you want other people to learn from your book?"

I ask this because we all have stories to tell. Stories of our lives and what we've been through as patients. Stories of our triumphs and our tragedies.

We could tell each other stories day and night and never finish!

But what makes a story truly useful, what Jesus demonstrates throughout the gospels, is that the story isn't about the teller. It isn't "listen to me because I've been through so much and I need you to admire that/be amazed by me."

The point of telling a story, of any ministry, is to draw people closer to God.

It's not about us. It's about him.

So, the next question I usually ask of a hopeful author is, "What do you want to teach others about? What useful things can they take away from your story?"

Notice in the gospels, Jesus doesn't boast of his miracles, wonderful though they are. In fact, on more than one occasion, he asks those he heals not to tell others about what he has done. Jesus' ministry is very definitely all about God, all about what is uplifting and divine.

When Jesus does condone speaking of a healing, he still puts the focus on the Lord and not himself as a human being. For example, in one occasion in chapter 5 of Mark's gospel, Jesus drives the demon Legion out of a man. When this man begs to accompany Jesus in his ministry, Jesus specifically tells him: "Go home to your family and announce to them all that the Lord in his pity has done for you" (Mark 5:1–20). Here, too, Jesus' ministry reveals him as the Son of God, but he doesn't self-aggrandize or boast of it.

In a world where fame, stardom, honors, and awards, not to mention misbehaving, are constant fixtures in the social vocabulary, humility is an underappreciated virtue. We gravitate toward the person who is the loudest, whose manner and message declare "Look at me!" Often, therefore, the person we are attracted by is less than stellar as a role model or example of upright living.

Yet, in our day, we have examples of people whose humility has propelled them to do great things, although perhaps not with the renown of some. Teachers, firefighters, priests, religious, physicians, nurses, stay-at-home parents—those who give their time and energy to helping others and who do not get much in return for it are truly heroes.

Another aspect of Jesus' healing that bears some consideration is the attitude of those whom he healed. The man freed from a demon was truly grateful, and even begged to go with the Lord. But others seem to have been more eager to receive the cure than to express appreciation for it afterward, as demonstrated in the story of the twelve lepers: All were cured, but only one came back to thank Jesus.

As Jesus continued his healing ministry, others who witnessed his miracles reacted adversely, too. When Jesus cured the man with a withered hand, for example, he did so on the Sabbath. This incensed the Pharisees, who then began to conspire with Herod's adherents to put Jesus to death (Mark 3:1–6).

When Jesus cured the man of the fierce demon, the people around him were so "seized with fear" (Mark 5:15) that they begged Jesus to leave them.

The more Jesus preached and healed, the more he met with disapproval from those in power—the truth of his ministry coming directly into conflict with the entrenched egos who could not recognize him because of their unwillingness to see.

As you move forward in your life, and as you recognize more clearly the path laid out for you by God, you will meet resistance, too. People you know and those you don't will have their own opinions of what you should be doing with your time and energy. They will be critical of you for a variety of reasons, sometimes even because they are jealous of your ability to develop drive and determi-

Jesus did not get paid in money for his ministry. He relied on the generosity of others for food, shelter, and the
simplest of clothing. He did not expect recompense for
his miracles, either. More than once, he asked people he
cured not to even tell others about what he had done to
help them.

- Do I expect to be paid back if I extend Christ's light to
  someone else?

nation while they themselves are still "deep in the mire" of self-pity
and victimhood.

In the moving pages of Mark's gospel, we see the clouds gather
above Jesus' ministry. We discover the disapproval that the Pharisees
and Herod's followers (and Herod himself) let fester, and which propelled them to plot against our Lord. We witness the lack of appreciation our Lord experienced from those he healed and those who saw
his healing and were fearful. And we understand that, on his human
journey, our Lord felt sorrow and loss.

The examples that Jesus sets for us about continuing to focus on
the Lord, continuing to reach out to others regardless of whether
they thank us or "pay us back," and the determination to forge ahead
through setbacks, trials, and rejection—all of these are inspiration for
us to continue.

The serenity and peace at the core of Jesus' behavior are freely available to us, too, even as clouds may gather around us and we find our
determination to continue "beyond pain" beginning to flag. Taking
our cue from the Lord and finding time to rest, pray, and renew, we
can have the energy we need to shine.

As our Lord told the disciples when the storm was raging all around
them: "Take courage, it is I, do not be afraid" (Mark 6:50).

Jesus,
I often get in the way of you
and doing your work.
Please help me to be more humble about
my abilities and place my trust squarely in you.
Erase my fear with your peace,
and grow my faith in you
so that you and not I lead my every step.
Amen.

Lazarus and Us

[Jesus said]: "This illness is not to end in death,
but is for the glory of God, that the Son of God
may be glorified through it."

JOHN 11:4

The story of Lazarus is powerful and encouraging. But it would be superficial for us to think that it is only about Jesus raising someone from the dead. From the beginning of chapter 11 of John's gospel we find a context and depth to the story that gives us great sustenance for our own journeys, no matter what stage of pain or illness we are in.

Lazarus was no stranger to Jesus. In fact, he was the brother of our Lord's two very good friends, Mary and Martha of Bethany. So, Jesus knew immediately who was ill when he received word from the sisters that Lazarus was ailing; our Lord's good friend was stricken.

Jesus' reply to the message of Lazarus' illness must have sounded very cryptic to the messenger: "This illness is not to end in death, but is for the glory of God, that the Son of God may be glorified through it" (John 11:4).

Again, from a superficial perspective, it sounds as if our Lord was sure that Lazarus would not die. The disciples and Mary and Martha might have believed this. But Jesus' pronouncement really referred to illness being a way to reflect the spirit and give witness and glory to God through Jesus' actions and presence.

Even after hearing of Lazarus' illness, Jesus did not immediately go to him. He waited two days before telling his disciples they would return to Bethany, in Judea.

So often, we pray for the pain to be taken away NOW, the medication to work NOW, the van driving us to the doctor's office to arrive NOW. We present our list of petitions to God along with a timeline. We are disappointed when things don't happen when and as we want them to happen. How human we are! As we see in the story of Lazarus, God works in his own time and in his own way. And when God does work, the result is not according to our own personal agenda, but according to the divine plan. As such, when we wait upon the Lord, we are walking closer with him, and not digging in our heels.

- How can I acquire greater patience, and thus lessen the stress I feel by demanding that things happen NOW?

- How can I arrange my day so that I spend more time in prayer with God, patiently listening for his guidance and his timing?

Jesus undoubtedly knew that Lazarus would die and that he, Jesus, would raise him from the dead. But he also knew that trouble awaited him in Bethany. His disciples reminded him, "Rabbi, the Jews were just trying to stone you, and you want to go back there?" (John 11:8).

Despite the potential peril, Jesus chose to continue his ministry and arrived in Bethany four days after Lazarus had been placed in the tomb.

A variety of reactions greeted Jesus when he approached and entered Bethany. Martha was the first to meet him, and she immediately and calmly acknowledged that Jesus was "the Messiah, the Son of God, the one who is coming into the world" (John 11:27). Others, however, were not so certain or calm.

Mary greeted Jesus with a group of weeping people. Others watching criticized him for not saving Lazarus: "'Could not the one who opened the eyes of the blind man have done something so that this man would not have died?'" (John 11:36).

Faced with such emotional suffering, and humanly realizing that his good friend Lazarus was dead, Jesus wept, too.

We can feel our Lord's pain because each of us has felt the ache of losing a loved one. The gaping hole in our lives and in our hearts never fully heals, and we mourn the loss of someone we love in every way.

A year after I was diagnosed with lupus, and when I was in a horrible flare and just beginning weekly chemotherapy, my brother, my only sibling, died suddenly. He died under unusual circumstances, and was on the opposite end of the country. I had so many questions, and very few answers—which is still the case to this day. All that made coping with his death that much harder.

After I got the news in a phone call from my mother, I discovered a last, unread e-mail he had sent me just prior to his death. I stared and stared at it. Seeing that e-mail and knowing it was the last time he'd tried to communicate with me was a kind of straw that broke open the floodgates of my sorrow. I've never wept so much—but I could produce no tears because of an eye condition related to my lupus that had affected my tear ducts. I couldn't sleep, even with a prescription that my rheumatologist provided to me.

The days that followed were agonizing both physically and emotionally. My lupus medication gave me horrible side effects of nausea, headaches, and fatigue, and my disease kicked into a worsened phase of flare.

Even worse than that, however, was the delay between when my brother died and when we could have the funeral Mass—more than two weeks. As I read the story of Lazarus in John's gospel, I could even in a small way relate to the sense of anticipation and then sorrow that Jesus might have experienced, waiting for those days between when he received word of Lazarus' illness and when he arrived in Bethany.

Before my brother's death I had attended many funerals of family members and friends. When we were finally able to celebrate the funeral Mass for my brother, however, it was the first time that I felt a tremendous sense of closure and hope. After more than two weeks of not knowing and not being able to see other family members, the Mass enveloped me in comfort and gave me strength. I was able to cry tears by that point, and I wept during the service. But my faith stirred within me, too, and I knew that our Lord was with each of us there at that time, and with my brother, too.

Jesus, of course, did more than weep with the others when he arrived in Bethany. He worked one of his most amazing miracles. He insisted that some in the crowd roll the stone from the mouth of the tomb, and commanded Lazarus to come out of it.

Lazarus did—alive and well, he came out of the tomb!

The story of Lazarus in John's gospel comes toward the end of Jesus' ministry. After the raising of Lazarus, some Jews in the Sanhedrin joined forces with the Pharisees and others who wanted to kill Jesus, and they began to finalize their plans. Jesus left Bethany and, according to John, "no longer walked about in public among the Jews, but he left for the region near the desert, to a town called Ephraim, and there he remained with his disciples" (John 11:54).

How cruel it seems that after Jesus raised a man from the dead, people would plot to kill Jesus!

Yes, cruel. But something more. "This illness is not to end in death, but is for the glory of God, that the Son of God may be glorified through it" (John 11:4).

I realize that I've put this quote in this chapter three times. There is a good reason for it. This statement is one of the most relevant to those of us who live with excruciating pain, overwhelming illness. When we are ill, we are called to live. That is, we are not called to wither away, isolated, alone, inactive. Our lives of illness and pain are excellent, even exquisite opportunities through which we can witness to God, spread his love, teach others to care, and show others who are ill that there is joy in any life, in all live.

For, recognizing God's glory brings joy.

Being able to extend comfort, to be of service to another brings joy.

Showing others that people who are ill are not relics brings joy.

You bring joy!

Yes! You bring joy!

Lazarus' poor, broken, sickened body perished under the hot, dry sun. But our Lord's light, brighter and life-giving, revived him.

We, too, broken and sickened, would weaken horribly, would waste away, if we did not nurture and treasure the life we have and the Spirit that fills us with hope and love.

And when our nurtured souls are focused on the Lord, we are also filled with light, and that light can be carried to others who need it.

And we bring joy!

Even the sickest individual has a valuable place in our society, although not everyone acknowledges it. The sickest of the sick and those most in pain teach the rest of us how to care. When we remind ourselves and others of this, we can educate, and enable care to become a part of living, a part of loving, a part of our witness to God.

When we live with chronic pain and illnesses, we will hear of someone with our condition, or a similar one, who dies from it. I often feel a bit shaken when I hear of someone dying of lupus, and of course I am sorrowful when I hear of a fellow patient I know succumbing to the disease.

At those times, however, I try to remember the remarkable things that person did and the way he or she made the most of life with pain. I resolve to take those examples into my own heart, and to try to be a good role model for other patients so that they, too, will not lose hope.

- How can I be a role model for others who suffer?

- Whom do I know who is sicker/in more pain than I am? How can I reach out to him or her today?

- What are the characteristics I most admire about others who suffer, and how can I adopt them myself?

We might think sometimes that it would be wonderful if Jesus were here today and would raise our departed loved ones from the dead, so they could live with us again here on earth. But we have something more than just that oh-so-human hope. We have faith.

As Jesus told Martha when he arrived in Bethany, "whoever believes in me will never die" (John 11:25).

The point of Lazarus, then, is more potent than the miracle of raising someone from the dead. It shows us what a gift our faith is. It illustrates for us that we are very precious in God's eyes. And it also reminds us that although illness, pain, and death are part of the human experience, we have God's promise of everlasting life. His promise is fulfilled in our Lord Jesus Christ.

Father,
please comfort me in my sorrow
at the losses I've experienced.
Give me the wisdom to know how
to care better for others,
and be a good role model for those who suffer, too.
Help me seek your light always,
and make of my pain
a living witness to you.
Amen.

Betrayal, Suffering, and Death

After withdrawing about a stone's throw from them and kneeling, Jesus prayed, "Father, if you are willing, take this cup from me; still, not my will but yours be done."

LUKE 22:41–42

In the Passion of our Lord, we see the fullness of Jesus' grace and strength in the face of suffering, betrayal, and death. How great is the responsibility on us to carry out our lives with even half of his determination and compassion!

First, Jesus shared the Last Supper with his apostles (Luke 22:1–34). He did so out of love, and yet he also knew that one at the table was about to betray him and another was going to deny knowing him.

How often do we withhold favors or kindness from people we believe have wronged us?

In the Garden, where he was arrested, one of Jesus' disciples "struck the high priest's servant and cut off his right ear." Jesus insisted that the disciples not retaliate and healed the servant's ear (Luke 22:47–53).

How often do we lash out at people who criticize us or attack us?

All through his sham of a trial and torture, Jesus could have cried out. We have already seen him express emotion at other times throughout his ministry—weeping at Lazarus' death, showing anger at the money-changers in the Temple. But when he was undergoing public, excruciating physical and personal pain, he did not weep or wail. He endured his suffering with such courage!

How often have we overreacted to our pain out of frustration that it exists or because we think we need to do so to get people to understand how bad we feel?

Jesus' mission was ordained from the beginning. He knew what he had to do. And he knew, too, that an element of strong character is to reflect dignity in everything, even in the experience of pain.

What, we might ask, can be dignified about suffering pain?

I have experienced numerous painful, very unglamorous tests in hospital settings. Even before the tests have begun, I've "suffered" the ignominy of having to wear those skimpy, ugly hospital gowns. I've been poked, prodded, scanned, stuck, and turned almost upside down.

Being dignified is one of the last things I think of when I consider these tests.

My illness and pain, too, don't seem to lend themselves to exhibiting dignity.

What is so dignified about having no hair? Getting nauseated every week because of my chemotherapy treatments? Having to endure neck spasms that render me incapable of sitting at the computer?

Where is the dignity in discussing very personal subjects in a clinical way with doctors?

If I look at my condition from the outside, I would be hard pressed to see it as dignified.

But if I look at my body from the inside, as a gift from God, and at my activities as part of the way the Lord wants me to live, then I start to see underneath the raw, crude nature of what I've just described and see that, as part of the human journey, all is imbued with dignity. It is only in my attitude, or in the attitudes of others, where dignity is denied.

For example, if I'm uncomfortable with not having hair, others will be uncomfortable, too. If I try to fight my chemo-induced nausea rather than treat it as best I can, I am bringing more stress on myself. If I look unkempt, slovenly and angry with the world, people will respond to me in kind or avoid me completely. If I bewail my constant pain, I create more stress, too, and get caught up in the pain itself rather than focus on positive ways to lessen it or remain active in spite of it.

Jesus endured suffering with divine grace as he walked along the torturous path to Calvary. What inner fortitude that took! If he had moaned and cried out with pain, or balked at carrying the cross, he would have taken the focus off the divine nature of his journey. It is so much more powerful to show divine, dignified behavior than to talk about it.

By his example of divine grace, Jesus also helps us see that the body is temporary, as is pain. It is the soul that lasts beyond this life, and our faith enables us to keep our souls healthy, even if our bodies are not.

- How do you express being in pain? Do you behave in a Christlike way?

- Do you ever go out of the house thinking, "It doesn't matter how I look because I feel terrible"?

The beauty of Holy Week is, to me, that we are able to reflect upon Jesus' truly human life before we celebrate the resurrection of Easter. And one of the key components of Jesus' life was that he died.

Death is a topic that many of us are not comfortable thinking about, let alone talking about. In many ways it is a mystery. We don't know when, how, or where each of us will die, whether we will be young, old, infirm, alone, or surrounded by loved ones. All we really know is that death comes to us all.

Jesus knew at the outset of his ministry that he would die. His particular death was horribly painful and public, and he knew that, too. In the Garden, he asked his Father in heaven that the "cup" would pass from him. That is, in his humanness, he had a moment of anxiety, a twinge of hesitation.

No doubt you have felt that way, too. I have. On the evening of my first colonoscopy/endoscopy/esophageal web dilation, I was ready to call off the procedures. I feared something would go wrong, they wouldn't be able to find a good vein for the IV, or they might find polyps or other evidence of another, serious health problem.

Still, I also knew that after the procedures, I should be able to eat much more easily (at least, until the web grew back). And, I hoped that I would have answers to questions about other problems that were occurring in the areas to be scoped and biopsied.

In the end (no pun intended!), the procedures did go well, although they had trouble finding a good vein, and I had two frightfully bruised and painful arms for about a month afterward from the failed attempts. But I still remember the fears from the evening before.

My experience was nothing like our Lord's in its severity or importance. As he waited in the Garden, praying for the cup to pass, he knew he was on a collision course with fulfilling God's promise, and he knew that the way would be agonizing. At the same time, he also knew that there would be joy in the resurrection, in the salvation of God's children. So, with this knowledge, our Lord was able to utter the second half of the prayer, "...still, not my will but yours be done."

It is for this point in our own lives that we strive—the understanding that God has a wonderful life chosen for us after our suffering on earth. Through our faith and with his guidance, we will get there. And, along the way, we will be able to shine with our faith upon others who are in need of comfort and hope.

In every way, Jesus was able to get "beyond pain," and know and show that it is all right to be human and to fear, but it is also important to focus our attention heavenward and desire and strive to do God's will throughout our lives.

- In what way are you fearful of your condition?
- How have you overcome fear in the past? How can you use those techniques now to overcome whatever fear you feel so you can submit fully to God's will for your life?

Also in the Garden were Jesus' disciples, minus Judas Iscariot, who was to betray him. After Jesus prayed alone, he discovered his good friends asleep. What friends these were! Our Lord had every right to be upset with them, and he did rebuke them, telling them to "get up and pray" (Luke 22:46). What a tremendous reminder for each of us—when we are most vulnerable, prayer is our strength and is very active.

Indeed, throughout our Lord's last days on earth, prayer was a centerpiece of both his ministry and his own life. At the Last Supper, he shared the vibrant gift of Eucharist and revealed how it is both action and prayer.

In the Garden, our Lord spent much time alone in prayer. Although that time was agonizing for him, he did not disconnect himself from conversation with his Father, but rather kept going and, finally, arrived at beautiful submission—"thy will be done." This action of total acceptance of what would happen to him in the next few days is awesome and shows how powerful prayer can be when we fully participate in it.

Jesus' admonition to his disciples to "get up and pray" encapsulates the active nature of prayer and the act of keeping an inner life going when outside forces are bearing down. "Get up," he tells his friends who are sleeping, oblivious to what is going on around them. "...And pray," he commands, so that his disciples will understand the divinity in the night and what is to come next. For our Lord, prayer is necessary for the journey and propels people forward rather than putting them to sleep!

We, too, benefit so very greatly from a prayer life that is active and comes along with us throughout our day. We are energized by uplifting prayer that takes in the glory of God's creation—the world. We are made wiser by prayer that includes active listening, truly yearning to hear God's will. We become courageous when we remember that our Lord accompanies us in our trials. He never sleeps!

Active prayer requires a desire to be fully focused and engaged in conversation with God. Sometimes, when we pray, we "rattle off" prayers so quickly that we lose the meaning of the words we are saying. Sometimes, too, we are so pressed for time that we don't allow God's voice to breathe into us deeply enough to understand what he is saying. In active prayer, the speed of praying is slower, so that the full weight of the words is felt to our very souls. Also, the timing of prayer is not limited by the numbers on a watch. We can actively pray and listen to God anywhere, just as he speaks to us anywhere, too.

Suggestion: Say the "Our Father" at your normal pace. Next, say it very, very slowly and think about each word that you utter.

From the Garden to Calvary, our Lord's suffering grew. He was humiliated, scourged, and burdened with the heavy wooden cross on which he would die. With each step, the crown of thorns on his head cut deeper and the road became more torturous. People mocked him, spit at him, denounced him. His ordeal would be impossible for most people to endure. Yet, not only did he endure it; he maintained his grace and ministry.

It amazes me that our Lord took his precious energy and love and poured it out on so many people on the way to Calvary! The gospels of Matthew, Mark, Luke, and John have slightly different descriptions of our Lord's Passion, but in all of them, his love shines forth!

Our Lord restored the ear of the high priest's servant after one of his disciples cut it off. Jesus provided for his mother, who stood at the foot of the cross (John 19:26–27) so that she would not be left without someone to watch over her after Jesus' death.

On the cross, Jesus extended his love to the criminal crucified with him: "Amen, I say to you, today you will be with me in Paradise" (Luke 23:42–43). He asked the Lord to forgive those crucifying him "for they know not what they do" (Luke 23:34).

Imagine forgiving those who are killing you!

In his last hours, nailed to a rough cross, Jesus provided an example of grace in suffering for all time. He was in the exact center of pain, the place of unspeakable torture in body, mind, and heart. Yet the clarity with which he spoke to others and ministered to them showed no inward focus, no self-pity, no afterthought.

Our Lord is the perfect example of looking and acting beyond pain.

In our humanness, we might think that we would never be capable of behaving even half as effectively and lovingly as Jesus. But I don't believe that God sent his Son to earth for us only to admire but not imitate. No, I think that Jesus' life shows us how, despite horrible trials, pain, setbacks, and even criticism and hatred, we can rise above. We can go beyond, because we have faith and because God dwells within us and his love inhabits our being.

So many patients I talk to say, "I don't believe God wants me to suffer. I don't believe he wants me to be in such pain. I know he wants me to be cured."

Actually, God wants us to be close to him and love him. He wants us to live lives of grace and truth, fellowship and compassion in good times and in bad.

Unlike in some parts of the Old Testament (remember Job?), where bad things were only supposed to happen to bad people, Jesus in the New Testament endows suffering with dignity, purpose, and grace. It is not the pain that is the point. Rather, the point is how a life with pain is lived, and how, through our examples, others can experience God's love.

Death comes to us all. Pain is a reality, sometimes a constant in many lives. Emotional disappointment, even betrayal, can affect us deeply.

But as we see in the life of Jesus, we can still pray. We can still act. We can still fulfill our purpose.

By the time Jesus' body was sealed in the tomb, his disciples, family, and friends turned to the Sabbath and mourning.

But as we know, three days later, Jesus' full purpose was revealed and with it, joy!

Jesus, you suffered and died for me.
I can scarcely understand the depth of your love,
but I am grateful to the core of my being.
In my waking and in my sleep,
Help me forge with you a stronger bond
so that I may meet my daily challenges
with grace, dignity, and love for others.
Amen.

Beyond Pain

[Jesus said to the disciples]: "Why are you troubled?
And why do questions arise in your hearts? Look at
my hands and feet, that it is I myself. Touch me and
see, because a ghost does not have flesh and bones as
you can see I have."

LUKE 24:38–39

Anyone who has endured a terrible ordeal could understand that, after his suffering and death on a cross, Jesus could very well have "taken time off" and stayed in heaven, apart from the people among whom he had walked as a man. But in fulfillment of Scriptures, and to show even more powerfully the love of the Father for his children on earth, our Lord rose and brought his presence to the disciples, breaking bread with them and inspiring them to go forth and spread the gospel.

This example of love shared and selfless giving brings to mind the importance of making the most of our "good days," when we have them, to help others as much as we can, and to witness to God's goodness and strength. Whether the "good days" are because we have been cured of our pain, or whether they are steppingstones across a river of physical challenges, each one is a gift to us and so can be a gift to others.

Some people I've spoken with have explained that on "good days" they try to forget the pain and suffering they've lived through. Or, they might hope that when they go on vacation, the illness or pain goes on vacation, too, and they can do all manner of breakneck activities because of this.

As I've discovered in my own life, however, once you have lived through a health ordeal and endured tremendous pain, the experience never really leaves you. It does not take a one-way flight, a permanent vacation. It leaves its mark in greater empathy, understanding, grace, patience, strength, and many other ways. The Gospel of Luke makes a point of our Lord showing his "hands and his feet" (Luke 24:40), indicating that the physical marks of Jesus' crucifixion were visible reminders of what he had endured only a few short days before appearing to the disciples.

Pain, once lived, is never forgotten. Nor are the lessons it imparts.

By your experience, you have much to give others. By your faith, you are called to reach out and share the Good News with others, too.

- How can you share the joy of the resurrection with others?

- What are the most important things you have learned about living with pain, and how can you share your lessons with others so that their lives are, even in small part, touched with comfort and wisdom?

Do you wish that you could have had someone give you at least a hint of what to expect when you first began to live with pain? Or, that someone could have held your hand, looked at you directly, and gently told you some way that you could fashion a life of meaning out of the ordeal you were about to go through?

If you did have someone like that in your life, you are truly blessed. But whether you did or did not enjoy the company of someone wise and caring, this much is true: You can be that person to someone else.

In Jesus' resurrection, we understand that God's presence in our lives and in our midst never goes away. By reaching out to his disciples after he rose, our Lord showed that his presence would be (and continues to be) active and everlasting.

Jesus didn't leave the harsh, painful world for his heavenly home— once he had died and had risen, he came back. And he gave back.

It was difficult, at first, for the men and women who loved Jesus to believe that he had truly risen from the dead. The first people Jesus encountered, as St. Luke writes, were incredulous. They couldn't believe they weren't seeing a ghost! In hindsight, we might think that we would never be so ignorant, that we would certainly recognize Jesus immediately and know fully the import of the resurrection. But hindsight is always a bit blinding, isn't it? We have the benefit of Scripture, of being able to see the whole gospel unfold page by page, verse by verse. We can reread passages until we understand them completely. We can take in all the seemingly small details and embrace them, too.

But the disciples were in the midst of the furnace of having seen Jesus tried, scourged, tortured, and crucified. They were afraid that they, too, would be rounded up, betrayed, and killed. They did not know what was to come, only what had happened, without the benefit of a written history or perspective.

As we contemplate what we have learned from pain, and what we continue to try to improve upon, sometimes we forget the details. Another benefit from sharing our knowledge and experience with others is that it can prompt within us a continuous feeling of appreciation and love for the Lord. Putting our suffering in context, for example remembering how we endured rough nights during a particularly hot and humid summer, can bring us more wisdom about how we can encourage others to better endure their trials.

One way that we can be sure to remember and share what we've learned is to keep a health journal, a kind of diary that documents the details of our pain. In a health journal, we can pour out our feelings, praises, prayers, and anger—and we can look back on the pages dotted with dried tears to see how far we've come and how much we have indeed learned that can be positive for ourselves and others.

> A health journal need not be fancy, expensive, or cumbersome. A simple spiral-bound notebook will do. Select a comfortable pen (so that at times of extreme pain, when you might grip it tightly, you don't exacerbate any pain in your fingers!). Keep the journal private so that you can feel you are communicating directly both with yourself and with God. Don't feel obligated to write everyday; write when you feel like it or jot a word or two if you just want to "touch base."
>
> Especially, celebrate your praises and successes!

When our Lord appeared to the disciples, he imparted another lesson learned from the pain of human living—we not only have much to teach others, but we can encourage others to carry the light of love and support forward, too.

Jesus said, "Thus it is written that the Messiah would suffer and rise from the dead on the third day and that repentance, for the forgiveness of sins would be preached in his name to all nations, beginning from Jerusalem. You are witnesses of these things. And [behold] I am sending the promise of my Father upon you; but stay in the city until you are clothed with power from on high" (Luke 24:46–49).

Clearly, Jesus was instructing the disciples to spread the gospel and not just keep the Good News to themselves.

In much the same way, by our caring example and enthusiasm, we can give others the desire to go forth, too. To go beyond their pain and suffering.

Can you imagine what an amazingly energized world it would be if we could infuse all who suffer with determination, compassion, and joy?

You might have noticed that I'm peppering my language about pain, suffering, and physical trials with seemingly opposing words such as "enthusiasm," "praise," and "joy." But as we build up our stamina, faith, and resolve, these positive outpourings of gratitude and hope will grow greater and shine more brightly.

The disciples themselves felt these things after Jesus appeared to them and gave them their instructions about how and when to proceed in their ministry. St. Luke writes: "As [Jesus] blessed them he parted from them and was taken up to heaven. They did him homage and returned to Jerusalem with great joy, and they were continually in the temple praising God" (Luke 24:51–53).

From the disciples' mourning came a morning of celebration. From their disbelief, fear, and confusion came clarity of emotion, thankfulness, and praise—all a direct result of the outpouring of Christ's love for them (and us).

A direct result of feeling God's love, support, and direction for us is the desire to praise him—to give thanks for his gifts. Sometimes, when we are in severe pain, this can be difficult to imagine. Yes, difficult, but not impossible.

We can praise even the smallest things in our lives, even if we lose sight of the "big picture" of how our lives are being molded by God. One of my favorite praise songs by African American gospel artist

Andraé Crouch starts out, "Lord, I thank you for the morning. Lord, I thank you for a brand new dawning. Lord, I thank you for another day to sing your praise."

So, we can begin our praise with a simple, "Good morning, Lord. Thank you for this day," and go from there. Even thanking God for the opportunity to praise him is praise, pure and simple.

- How can I thank God today?
- How can I praise God today?

Praise can also include lifting up our hands to heaven in supplication and thanks. It can be as easy as admiring a delicate flower by the roadside, or looking with awe at the play of clouds against the sky.

Praise can be a silent "thank you!" for having the strength to open a tightly sealed jar in the kitchen!

I express gratitude to God each time I put on one of my wigs—what gifts they are! And I try to remember to thank others for their friendship and support—also a way to praise God.

As we praise God for the seemingly small things, we begin to understand that they are not small at all, but rather part of the large world in which God has placed us. We matter in this world. We move about in it, and we make a difference.

We, in our pain, have much to offer others and much to do to reflect God's light and love.

Truly, when I get started praising God, it's very difficult to get me to stop!

At some point in our lives with pain and illness, we will dwell on the subject of death. For many, this is a wretched topic and a feared eventuality. In today's world, we hear discussions of "assisted suicide" becoming more accepted in some corners of the world, and we also hear people weigh "quality of life" against a cheapened value of life itself.

We of faith know that life is made up of more than what perceived "quality" might be present at any given moment. And we know that death is not an end, but rather part of our journey.

- Do you ask God to end your suffering? Or, do you ask him for ways to endure it while keeping you close to him?

- What does "quality of life" mean to you?

- Spend a few days praying over God's gift of life and what it means to you, no matter the perceived quality of it to others.

Through Jesus' death and resurrection, we have hope, light, and the promise fulfilled that, when we think of eternity in heaven, can make our lives of suffering seem brief and endurable.

As our Lord walked those agonizing steps to Calvary, he did not request to be carried along. He suffered each step. As he hung on the cross, he did not pray that death would come quickly. He let time pass as it was supposed to.

Jesus endured his pain, died and rose!

As with the disciples, the reality of the resurrection can infuse in us a resolve and energy that transcend pain, go beyond suffering. With our faith as a guide, we can dispel the darkness that surrounds discussions of "quality of life," and shine light on the preciousness of life itself, at all ages and all stages, knowing that this world is not the end, nor is death.

We're all aiming for heaven! What praise there is in that!

O Lord, Light of my life,
as I move farther from a self-centered sufferer
to a praiseful, active witness to you,
help me to demonstrate
in deed and communicate in word
how true is your promise,
how real is the resurrection,
and how awesome is your love.
Amen.

Comfort for All

[Jesus told the disciples]:
"Blessed are the poor in spirit,
for theirs is the kingdom of heaven.
Blessed are they who mourn,
for they will be comforted.
Blessed are the meek,
for they will inherit the land.
Blessed are they who hunger and thirst
for righteousness,
for they will be satisfied.
Blessed are the merciful,
for they will be shown mercy.
Blessed are the clean of heart,
for they will see God.
Blessed are the peacemakers,
for they will be called children of God.
Blessed are they who are persecuted
for the sake of righteousness,
for theirs is the kingdom of heaven.
Blessed are you when they insult you and persecute you and

*utter every kind of evil against you [falsely] because of me.
Rejoice and be glad, for your reward will be great in heaven.
Thus they persecuted the prophets who were before you."*

MATTHEW 5:3–12

Many Jews in Jesus' time were waiting for a Messiah who would be a powerful warrior, vanquishing all enemies and establishing a tangible kingdom on earth. When our Lord presented the Beatitudes, I wonder if some of the disciples, who were Jewish, thought that Jesus was referring to a soon-to-be kingdom on earth, where those who were oppressed would suddenly be lifted up to positions of wealth, power, and dominion? Certainly, I've spoken with fellow believers who have hoped or believed that the Beatitudes refer to earthly reward for being poor, meek, or otherwise downtrodden. Some of them become more and more despondent as life—and pain—go on without relief, without reward for the days and nights of suffering. Some go so far as to feel cheated and, thus, turn their backs on their faith.

Let's consider the Beatitudes within the context of the whole gospel, including our Lord's death and resurrection, however, and see with greater clarity that Jesus is really acknowledging that those who suffer, who remain "clean of heart," will be rewarded in heaven. When we do this, the Beatitudes become even more potent in their meaning. Here, rewards do not come in the form of a plaque, a plot of land, or a commendation from a person or institution. These rewards are given by God for eternity!

The Beatitudes are a joyful statement of finding good through adversity and God-focused strength when others persecute us.

As we have seen in Jesus' example, the more we suffer, the more we walk in Jesus' roughened, agonizing footsteps to Calvary, the closer we are to our Lord. If we never suffered in this life, we would have no understanding of the great sacrifice and love our Lord had and still has for us.

Jesus mourned.

Jesus was persecuted.

Jesus strove to be a peacemaker.

Jesus was poor.

Jesus was merciful.

Jesus was all of these things and more. He showed us the way to eternal life, and the Beatitudes are a beautiful summary of how God lifts the lowly and how God loves each of us.

Another aspect of the Beatitudes that is problematic to some is that Jesus says, after enumerating all of the "blessings," "Rejoice and be glad, for your reward will be great in heaven."

Rejoice if we're poor? Meek? Hungry for righteousness? Insulted and persecuted? Rejoice if we mourn?

Each of the things that Jesus mentions is a harsh reality of humanity. I don't think he intends for us to "do the happy dance" just because we are down, ailing, or insulted. But I do think that he wants us to understand that these, like all suffering on earth, are finite.

Our reward, and the end to suffering, is in heaven.

Just as moving beyond a focus on pain can open up a life of opportunity, meaning, and joy, so too can this knowledge that God offers us eternal salvation. No matter the depth and breadth of our earthly trials, in heaven there is only rejoicing!

 As a daily prayer, read the Beatitudes slowly, asking God to inspire you anew through his love and hope.

Chronic pain can wear us down and make us feel very limited. Energy, potential, hope, humor—each of these things and more can seem bottled up inside of us as pain keeps us physically confined and emotionally stunted.

Another of the beautiful gifts given us in the Beatitudes is the acknowledgment of our earthly limitations and our unlimited eternal reward, bestowed on us by our loving heavenly Father. When we understand that the pain we have now is earthly and our trial finite, we can shift our feelings of limitation to a smaller corner of our conscious focus. We can open our hearts to the unlimited love and light God gives. Even if we are bed-bound and physically alone, our souls can soar!

The full import of the Beatitudes was probably lost on the disciples when Christ first presented them. They had not yet witnessed the awful suffering our Lord would endure, nor did they yet understand what eternal salvation meant. But still our Lord planted these early seeds of the Beatitudes; as his suffering unfolded, the disciples could better grasp his divinity and the awesome grace of salvation, and understand more fully just what "blessed" really meant.

As we allow each of the words of the Beatitudes to take root in us, we can cultivate our souls and know more deeply that earthly suffering has a purpose and our reward, glorious and grand, is in heaven.

Lord,
at the times I feel most earthbound in pain,
hold me up and comfort me.
In the moments when I feel most vulnerable,
let your words of hope nurture my soul
and help me understand how blessed I am, indeed.
And please bestow your wisdom upon me,
that I may truly rejoice and be glad.
Amen.

JESUS—FOOD FOR THOUGHT

Here are some questions to consider with others or on your own:

1. Have I consciously acknowledged the importance of humility when it comes to living with pain? How can I better take the focus off of "me" and begin to see Christ's light in others?

2. When was the last time I did something for someone else? Did they repay me in any way? If not, how did I feel about that? How did Jesus react to people who said, "thank you," and those who did not?

3. How do I plan for activities so that I can prepare for possible upsets or unexpected problems? Have I ever set myself up to fail at doing an activity?

4. Consider the meanings of "to cure" and "to heal." How do you feel about the possibility that your pain might continue throughout your life? Where are you on the path to accepting that God's will be done with regard to your pain?

5. What are the things that tempt you the most to remain in your "discomfort zone" of lonely pain? Given Christ's example of his temptation in the desert, how can you better resist those temptations and gain strength and courage?

6. How important is it to you that everyone you know accept your health status as you present it? Is your reliance on the opinions of others important to you? Why or why not?

7. Do you take enough time to rest, pray, and rejuvenate your body and soul? How can you better tend to your need for "down time," and learn to say "no" to things that sap your energy, drive, and health?

8. What gives you a sense of dignity? How can you keep it close by in medical settings, or throughout your regular daily routine?

JOY

Finding Purpose

There are different kinds of spiritual gifts but the same Spirit; there are different forms of service, but the same Lord; there are different workings but the same God who produces all of them in everyone. To each individual the manifestation of the Spirit is given for some benefit. To one is given through the Spirit the expression of wisdom; to another faith by the same Spirit; to another gifts of healing by the one Spirit; to another mighty deeds; to another prophecy; to another discernment of spirits; to another varieties of tongues; to another interpretation of tongues. But one and the same Spirit produces all of these, distributing them individually to each person as he wishes.

1 CORINTHIANS 12:4–11

Through the examples of Job and Jesus, we are able to see how pain is not the beginning and end of our human experience. We learn how there can be a purpose for tremendous suffering that can bring great reward. We discover how it is possible to nurture lives of meaning with, and in spite of, pain, and to encourage, support, and inspire others. We see how our loving Father wishes for us to bring light and be a light to the world, no matter what our physical capabilities might be.

Moreover, through the examples of Job and Jesus, we know how true joy comes after suffering, mourning, and despair.

So, we can with a loud and enthusiastic voice say "Yes!" to moving beyond our own pain. We can say "Yes!" to following God's will for our lives, his will that is not focused on our health challenges, but rather on what positive, uplifting things we make of them.

We say "Yes!"…to what?

As we read through the passage from 1 Corinthians, with which I began this section, we see that each of us has individual gifts of the Spirit. They are clearly listed in Paul's letter. What is not listed is which individual gets which gift.

How can we know what the special purpose is for each of us?

Woven throughout this section focused on joy are suggestions for ways to deepen and define our discernment of God's will. I can't give you answers—you will have to find those yourself. But I can offer some food for thought and exercises that might assist you in assessing your life, talents, and gifts and how you might make use of them, beyond pain, now and in the future.

Are you ready? Yes!

☙ Taking Stock

One of the ways to start discerning God's purpose is to take stock of your individual talents and abilities. Are you a good communicator? Well-organized? Intuitive? Do you know what people are going to say before they say it?

What social skills come most easily to you? What do you do better than most people?

What activities have you done in the past that have given you the greatest, deepest feeling of accomplishment and happiness? (Not material happiness, but rather the feeling that you have done something good and made a difference.)

Taking stock is not the same thing as counting the diplomas on your wall. So many of our talents are "intangible," the kind of talents we can't count so much as count on. These include being compassionate, having a good sense of humor, knowing the right words to say to someone who suffers, being able to defuse tense or angry situations. They are also attributes such as being on time, dependable, and exhibiting grace under pressure. They are the things you do in a positive way that are uniquely and endearingly you—the things that reflect the good of God's creation.

As you take your skills inventory, also note the tangible things you have accomplished in the past because of your gifts. Did you right a wrong? Bring forgiveness full circle? Help someone get back up on his or her feet, financially, emotionally, or otherwise?

Taking stock of gifts has to be an honest process. This is not the time to sugarcoat what you are capable of. It's also not a time to mourn the loss of opportunities. Rather, it is a time to truthfully acknowledge the unique gifts God has given you and that you could use in fulfilling his purpose for you.

❧ Listen to Others

As adults, we're past the time of getting comments on our report cards ("Plays well with others," for example). But we still receive feedback from others, and this should be folded into our time of taking stock, too. Sometimes, we are so close to situations that we cannot see clearly the impact we have. So listen to others and what they perceive as your gifts. Listen, too, to the criticism and decide what is valid (remember, this is a time for honesty!) and what can be discarded.

As you receive input from others, match this up with what you've thought about your strengths. Recognize patterns or what made certain situations more successful than others. Begin to think of ways that you can practically and positively use your gifts in the future, when you've decided what activities you are going to take part in as you move beyond pain-focused living.

Read and Re-read Scripture

Job is but one example in the Old Testament of people who suffered greatly, but who found joy after all. As you move along in your discernment process, read and reread Job and other stories, taking note of the character traits and manifestations of God's will unfolding in each life.

In the New Testament, read the gospels slowly, closing your eyes and envisioning Jesus' life, teaching, and especially the times when he experienced pain. More than 2,000 years have passed since he walked as a man on earth, but he is still so very present to us!

Also, read Acts and the other books of the New Testament. The disciples suffered greatly for their faith, and even died because of it. But they carried out their ministry with determination, jubilation, and compassion. Think about how they traveled and taught despite the animosity toward them, and let their courage inspire you to strengthen yours.

Be Prepared for Subtleties

For most of us, discerning God's will for our lives does not involve a "Moses Moment," when we suddenly hear, clearly and for good, God's voice telling us exactly what we should do. No, when we are in the ongoing process of discernment, we have to be prepared for the subtle ways that God directs, redirects, and gently nudges us in the direction he wants us to go.

Almost all my life, I thought I wanted to be a writer. I moved to Los Angeles to attend UCLA's prestigious School of Theater, Film, and Television and earned a Master of Fine Arts in Theater Arts, with a concentration in writing. I thought I'd be writing scripts in Hollywood.

God had other plans!

Although I had clearly discerned that I had a gift for communication, especially for writing, I had not clearly discerned what I would be writing about. It wasn't until I was diagnosed with lupus that the purpose of the gift became clear and I realized that my life experiences, gifts of the Spirit, and desire to do God's will all came together in the ministry in which I joyfully find myself now.

Truly, in my life, discerning God's purpose came not out of one success after another, but out of the crucible of nearly dying from a lupus flare and having to stop nearly all other activity while I fought it with faith and my medical team.

So, as you move through your discernment process, be prepared for the subtle ways that God encourages you (or moves you from one place to another). Often, he speaks in a quiet whisper that can only be heard when we're deep in listening prayer, a most vital part of moving beyond pain to the joy that comes from carrying out God's purpose in each of our lives.

O Father in heaven,
You have given me so very much.
Please help me to see and understand your many gifts
And trust that you have a purpose for my life
That is more than focused on pain—
it is focused on you!
Amen.

The Praying Spirit

Lord, give me a praying spirit,
a praying spirit.
Lord, help me to say "yes."

FROM "A PRAYING SPIRIT" (ELBERNITA CLARK)

The words I've quoted here come from a song that I and my choir used to sing at Mass on Sundays. It's one of the gems in the African American Catholic hymnal, "Lead Me, Guide Me." The words are very simple, but so very true. Each time I pray, I hope I have a praying spirit and ask that the Lord will help me to say "yes" to him.

In our society today, it is not easy to have a praying spirit. We're bombarded by noise, responsibilities, extraneous distractions, and a pace of living that leaves us breathless and exhausted. Carving out even five minutes to pray, when all is quiet and we have the energy and dedication to be with God alone, can seem impossible.

Yet without significant prayer time, we will be consumed by external concerns at the expense of building a strong, deep, and abiding relationship with God. We will not benefit from the grace of prayer, nor will we be able to move ahead in our pursuit of doing God's will.

Through prayer, we are able to relax with our Father, who is all-knowing and all-loving. We can bring out insecurities, fears, failings, and confusion and know that he does not judge us for them, but takes them upon his own shoulders, thus allowing us to stand taller and move ahead.

In prayer, too, we can practice the wonderful gift of our faith, the prayers and traditions passed down to us. Through these, we connect with the Church beyond the confines of our room, or even our sickbed, and unite with others in solidarity and compassion. Somewhere in the world, right now, there are people we don't even know praying for each of us. What a wonder and a joy that is!

Prayer allows our spirits to breathe, something that is greatly needed but challenged by the world as a whole. We can drink in quiet like parched travelers and afterward feel refreshed and renewed—and ready to tackle whatever the rest of the day or night holds!

So, how can we put on more of a praying spirit today? Here are some suggestions:

Pray as an Adult

When we were young, it was usually our parents who introduced us to prayer. At bedtime, for example, we would kneel beside the bed and pray for the people (and perhaps pets) we wanted God to bless. At mealtime, we would say grace, often quickly because we were hungry and eager to get to the food.

As we prepared for the sacraments, we were introduced to more prayers, beautiful prayers, and memorized them. Perhaps we received a Rosary for First Eucharist, or a Catholic prayer book for confirmation.

These early lessons in prayer served as a firm foundation in our early Catholic formation. But, for some, the foundation remains all that is built of an adult approach to prayer. And, as life moves on and problems, conflicts, and catastrophes arise, sometimes the memorized prayers seem inadequate.

We hunger for more of a deep spirituality, a deep connection with God.

When I was very young, and very ill, my mother gave me an indispensable gift. She told me that no matter how alone I was, or how sick, I could always talk to God. He was always with me, everywhere, and it didn't matter if it was daytime or nighttime.

So, talk to God I did.

I learned all the childhood prayers, but I also did a lot of "just talking." Like most children, I did very little listening, but the talking was helpful, especially at times when I was frustrated, sad, or confused.

Now I understand that talking to God also needs to be mixed with listening. If we only talked to God, all we would hear is our own voice. And when it comes to discernment of purpose, we really need to hear God's voice more than our own.

The prayers we learned as young Catholics are still very valid and vital. As adults, we can add to them our own "talking to God," as well as listening in quiet and with focus to God's whisper and wisdom. In this way, we can have a very grown-up, strong spirituality to meet all the challenges, including living with pain that comes our way. And we will be able to experience joy that is mature and soul-deep.

Now what, you might ask yourself, am I going to do about finding the time?

♨ Consciously Schedule Prayer Time

Our doctors give us medication to take on a schedule, and we have to make specific appointments to see them. We schedule other activities, too, such as dates, vacations, bedtime, or watching favorite television programs.

Why not schedule in some prayer time?

If you find that your prayer time is being crowded out by other activities, people or your pain, make a conscious effort to pencil in on your calendar blocks of time when you will pray. Honor that time, as you would a doctor's appointment, even going so far as to take the telephone off the hook to avoid distractions. If anyone questions your actions, explain to them that you need this time.

And you do!

You need prayer time in order to have the inner strength to forge ahead each day and be able to rest calmly each night.

You need prayer time as you need time to eat, take your medication, or talk to loved ones.

You need the time. So schedule it. And honor it.

❧ Set Yourself Up to Succeed

For many pain sufferers, mornings and evenings are the most difficult times of day/night.

In the morning, stiffness, aches, and the morning routine conspire to make such simple tasks as brushing one's teeth difficult. In the evening, accumulated pain from the day's activities (or inactivity) can interfere with reading, relaxing, and prayer.

When you select your time to pray, consider how you feel and how much energy you have. Give yourself as much room for success as you can: If you set yourself up to fail—for example, if you are too fatigued to think clearly, let alone listen to God—then you will only be disappointed.

When it comes to praying, there's no "right" or "wrong" time. Choose the time that's best for you—and go for it!

❧ Vary Your Prayer

Jesus gave us the cornerstone prayer of our faith—the Our Father—and we can benefit from it each time we pray it, whether as a community or alone. The Rosary and other prayers are wonderful expressions of faith and can center us as we strive to focus on God and leave our distracting, confounding lives outside for the duration of our prayer time.

But it's also important to practice listening prayer, where our minds and hearts are stilled, cleared of all our petitions and words and worries, and we are able to just sit in God's presence. It is here that we can feel our souls filled up with God's love and comfort, and here that we can begin and continue our process of discernment.

One of the things that helps me listen in prayer (especially on days when my mind is occupied with, for example, waiting for the latest lab results) is to use a phrase that will bring me back to listening if I'm distracted. If my mind wanders, I might begin to pray, "Lord, I'm really listening," and repeat that phrase a few times to get back to my focus.

Or I might change my posture or sitting position, settle into the new attitude, and consciously clear my mind of distractions so that I can more fully pay attention to inner quiet.

It's very important to remember that God loves us and wants us to reach out to him as often as we can. So, in prayer, we can relax, as if we're with a very good friend, and just be still. And listen.

Prayers of Praise

Sometimes we forget that words of thanks, appreciation, and praise are prayers, too. In our daily lives, we need not confine all of our prayer to an isolated place and time; we can "check in" with God whenever we wish. Commenting on the beauty of a flower, the brightness of a day, or the quick movement of traffic when we're eager to get from point A to point B—all of these are a form of prayer that gives thanks to God. What's more, they help us look outside of our limited scope to enjoy and comment upon the world around us.

The more we praise God, the more we're lifting up our appreciation and joy at being part of his creation—a good way to coax us out of our pain focus if it's a particularly difficult day.

Some of the Psalms are beautiful prayers of praise that extol God's greatness, majesty, and might. If you're ever at a loss for words to pray, read Psalms, taking the words slowly and to heart.

♨ Make Music

For me, music is a powerful addition to other ways and forms of prayer. When I'm at a total loss for words, or feel an emotion welling up inside me that I can't quite define, music can be a soothing balm and a rousing witness. Do you ever feel like just bursting into song? Don't be shy! Lifting our voices is a very real way to pray, praise, and participate in life. And, as God is our all-loving Father, there is no reason to be embarrassed if you think you cannot carry a tune. "Make a joyful noise" is a phrase that pertains to us all!

♨ The Spirit of Prayer

As we deepen and widen our prayer experience, we begin to crave that communication and conversation with God all the more. Praying becomes a joy-filled pursuit that feeds our need to nurture our spirit and give us sustenance for our earthly journey. We want to pray more—and we do.

Through words and quiet, music and marvel, we grow in strength, wisdom and grace the more we pray. We also arrive ever more surely and joyfully at the one, small word that resonates profoundly throughout our lives: Yes!

O Lord,
when I was a child,
I prayed like a child.
Now, in my adulthood, help me to
pray more closely and listen more deeply
to your word and your will.
Lord, help me to say "yes" always.
Amen.

Dream Often, Dream Deeply

When I was a child, I used to talk as a child,
think as a child, reason as a child;
when I became a man, I put aside childish things.

1 CORINTHIANS 13:11

There is no doubt that knowing purpose is a powerful motivator to act beyond pain, and that taking stock of talents and gifts is one of the important steps to this discernment. Building a strong relationship with God, especially through prayer, is essential to nurturing spiritual depth and inner peace, as well as allowing God to guide each step of the way.

But there is another aspect of moving beyond pain that cannot be overlooked. Indeed, it should be nurtured along with talents, prayer, and listening to God because it is integral to one of the most amazing gifts in our lives: imagination.

Without using our imaginations, we would probably not go far beyond the confines of what we concretely know as real, even if it is painful. We would hesitate to venture into an unfamiliar place or try our hand at a new activity or skill. We wouldn't be able to connect our painful now with a future potential.

We wouldn't be able to make our dreams come true.

So often, pain has a way of wearing us down to the bare bone, to the place where we don't believe that anything uplifting, positive, or even fun is possible. We might shy away from dreaming at all because health challenges have shattered what dreams we had. We cannot imagine anything less than suffering in the future.

But God would not have given us the gifts we have (remember the list of gifts you made while reading the first section of this part on joy?) if he didn't want us to use them. And he wouldn't have put the desire in our hearts to accomplish something for his kingdom unless he wanted us to go all out.

Our gift of imagination is an integral part of moving from "start" to "go."

﹖ We Were Children, Once

When we were young, we might have dreamt of being a beautiful princess, flying comic book hero, or strong and courageous firefighter. As we grew older, we might have imagined being able to live on a deserted island, travel to a distant planet, or discover dinosaur fossils in the backyard. Often, our play centered around our dreams; we made up elaborate stories and acted them out with makeshift costumes and props. Perhaps all the children in the neighborhood joined in, creating our own little world within a world we had barely begun to understand.

What has happened to those dreams?

We learned that we were not a princess, a comic book hero, or a firefighter. There were no dinosaur fossils nearby. We were far from being able to reach a deserted island.

Did we become disillusioned with dreaming and shelve the whole exercise?

If so, we need to take it off the shelf, dust it off, and reacquaint ourselves—we who are now adults—with the positive practice of dreaming.

For us, living with pain and a myriad of constraints, dreaming is not meant to take us away from our troubles, but rather it is a tool to draw us closer to our purpose. In the comfort of our homes, with no judgments or constraints, we can dream—that is, imagine—how we can take the gifts God has give us and use them enthusiastically, joyfully, to move us beyond pain and into the world.

When I work with my fellow patients in workshops, I invite them to imagine something that they've either always wanted to try to do, or used to do before pain and illness stopped them.

What was it about the activity that attracted you to it? What was it that you really liked about doing it?

Why do you think you can't do it today?

I mentioned that I'd always wanted to be a writer and thought that was where God was leading me. But when I was diagnosed with lupus, for a time I was incapable of thinking of myself as a productive writer because I thought the avenues I used to have were forever closed to me. What a revelation it was when I realized that there was another avenue that was so much more of a fit with my life, skills, and desire to serve!

A Dream of One's Own

In your life, think of something you've dreamed of doing. There must be something personal that draws you to it—a dream must be between you and God, not something that others say you must do.

What stops you, now, from pursuing your dream? Are your reservations valid?

Use your imagination as you explore your dreams. Examine a dream from all angles and research how others have achieved what you would like to do. Try to turn off the "can't" voice inside of you, that pessimism that can stop you in your tracks. For example, perhaps you are bedridden but want to participate more fully in the life of your parish. You've thought that, with your gifts of compassion, organization, and time, you could start up a telephone or Internet prayer circle. But there isn't one at your parish, and you don't think there ever has been one.

Do you let "never" stop you? Dream! Use your imagination! Talk to the pastor and others in the parish. If God has put this on your heart, there will be a way—but you cannot wait until the opportunity drops into your lap!

Dreams can change, but the essence of a dream is often very much the same from childhood to adulthood. For someone who dreamt of being a flying comic book hero, perhaps it was not so much the cape and the calamities, but rather the ability to save others from harm that was appealing. As an adult suffering from chronic pain, you know you cannot jump off of a building and fly to the rescue. But you could use your experience to inspire and encourage others who despair. You could reach out to people who feel their lives are hopeless.

You could save others—by bringing them to Christ!

Using Our Adult Heads and Childlike Hearts

In childlike wonder, we can imagine a dream in all its beauty and joy. The benefit of dreaming as an adult is that we are also practical (most of the time). We can take a fluid, pie-in-the-sky dream and break it down into doable steps, action plans, and goals to meet along the way.

Blending practicality with dreaming is a powerful combination, as if you are actually baking that dish you craved when you read the recipe in a cookbook.

Using that recipe analogy, picture the "finished masterpiece," the goal you wish to achieve. Make a list of the ingredients you need, creatively finding substitutions for one or more of them if the original ingredients are unavailable. If, for example, you cannot travel to the workplace, consider making the workplace come to you via the Internet or telephone.

If you only have one "good" hour in the day, arrange your schedule so that you can make optimal use of it.

If you cannot afford full-time tuition, investigate community colleges or online options to learn the material you want to master.

"Where there's a will, there's a way," is not a cliché—it's a fact!

⸙ You Have Time—Use It!

Any good chef will tell you that mastering a difficult recipe takes trial and error. So it is with fulfilling a dream and living out your purpose. Our Lord lived at home for thirty years before he embarked on his ministry full time. Job suffered greatly for days before he realized his purpose and was able to move beyond pain.

Whether it takes you years or days, keep dreaming, imagining, praying, and planning. Listen to God's voice, honestly and completely.

You can do it!

Jesus,
you show me the way to eternal life.
Show me also the way to be a witness to you,
to be of service to others,
to be fully alive in your great world.
Guide my thoughts and my dreams,
And keep me close to you.
Amen.

Seeing and Believing Beyond Pain

[Jesus said to Thomas]: "Have you come to believe because you have seen me? Blessed are those who have not seen and have believed."

JOHN 20:29

Perhaps by now you have an idea of where God is leading you. Through prayer, you have discerned a way that you can leave behind a life focused on pain and forge ahead to a life of great meaning and service.

Perhaps, inside, a voice begins to drown out your resolve. Perhaps it says:

"I could never do that!"

"But, even if I do [activity], I'll never feel better."

"My life can't improve unless the pain goes away."

"No one wants to be around a sick person anyway."

"Why me? Why not someone else, Lord?"

In the years since I became part of a community of pain-racked patients, I've heard these arguments against action—and more.

It is easy for those who suffer to believe that pain is the only reality in life because it can be so overwhelming. We lose belief in our ability to do anything more than be a victim.

Yet, others have overcome disbelief and victimhood. They have taken their pain and fashioned from it lives of purpose, meaning, and joy.

If you've prayed, imagined, dreamt, and planned, and you still seem skeptical, there might be one thing that you need to adopt, or strengthen, in your arsenal of gifts.

Faith.

Faith in Action

A stunning example of how faith lifts us up and beyond earthly concerns is in the account of "doubting Thomas," as told in the Gospel of John.

Knowing that Jesus rose from the dead gave the disciples immense resolve, energy, and joy. They saw and believed that Jesus rose.

Thomas, however, was not present at Jesus' initial appearance to the rest of the disciples. He heard the tales of the resurrection, but doubted Jesus could have risen from the dead. It was only when our Lord appeared to Thomas, and Thomas probed the wounds in Jesus' hands and side that he believed.

Many of us, at various times, can relate to Thomas! How tempting it is to refuse to believe something unless we see it with our own eyes, or to doubt we're capable of doing something unless we can do so overnight and with no obstacles to thwart us.

How easy it is to refuse to engage in a particular activity, however much we want to, unless we have ironclad guarantees that we're going to be all right and the activity is going to be a success.

How easy it is to lack trust in a body that has let us down so many times before!

Jesus' reaction to Thomas is reassuring for us who sometimes lack belief. He suffers Thomas' skepticism, and then reminds him (and us) that, "Blessed are those who have not seen and have believed."

Jesus loves Thomas, and he loves us. He loves those who have doubted and then believe, and he loves those who believe, purely and simply.

What does this mean for us, who wish to go beyond our pain into lives rich with faith, meaning, and joy?

🐾 When in Doubt…

Because of his skepticism, Thomas could not participate in the other disciples' joy. He was held back because of his doubt and because of his ego. (I cannot imagine demanding that our Lord appear to me and show me his hands and his side to prove he is risen!) Thomas demanded proof, a sure thing, before he would believe. Poor Thomas!

We, too, through human skepticism, can be kept from thinking we can do something, be something, besides patients with broken bodies. We can limit our vision to the foot of our bed, and miss out on the joy experienced by other sufferers, who have found a way beyond.

We can also doubt that we are capable of feeling joy because: 1) we are in pain and pain is joyless, or 2) we felt joy, once, and it was nothing like any of the emotions coursing through our lives now.

The first point first:

Yes, pain in and of itself is "joy-less," meaning we aren't elated because we suffer. But when we start to see a purpose in pain, and when we think of the ways in which we can still act and move and carve out lives of meaning with and in spite of it, the entire *experience* of pain can bring a profound joy in our resilience, creativity, resolve, and strength.

The second point, I think, is what can hold us back even more from putting on joy in our lives of pain.

So often, our society tells us that joy, as with other "positive" emotions, is a palpable rush of energy and glee that carries us away to some state of euphoria. Joy, then, to the secular world, is an almost physical emotion, a feeling that sparks and burns fiercely. Moreover, it is something that is personal, proprietary, and self-centered. As with happiness, we pursue joy, feel joy, are filled with joy.

Joy, then, to many people, is a thing that's felt "all or nothing."

If we believe, in our own lives, that for us to feel joy, we have to be in a constant state of giddiness, then we will miss out on the more faith-centered meaning of joy.

❧ Joy Is More than Skin Deep

Joy, to the disciples, was what motivated them to go forth after our Lord revealed his resurrection to them. It was what came after a storm and stayed close in their hearts as they spread the gospel. It accompanied Paul's greetings to the early Christians, as he wrote often of the "joy" he felt when he thought of the strong faith they exhibited.

Joy, to us, is more than a fleeting emotion. It takes root in our appreciation for the many gifts of God and burns warmly in our hearts as we contemplate our worth in his eyes.

Joy is also something very active and is not meant to be kept to ourselves. Joy is one of the ways that we can find the energy and courage within to be able to venture out into the world—to dare to dream and do.

If we thought that by moving beyond our pain, we would only experience more pain, we would understandably not dare to budge. But if we have faith in our Lord and understand how he loves us, we know joy is possible and that our joy can illuminate other, darker corners of the world.

❧ What Has Worked Counts

One of the most effective ways to draw out joy in hearts trampled by oppressive pain is to think of past achievements and present blessings. Each of us has overcome great hurdles in the past and become stronger for it. Each of us has achieved something that was hard-won.

Perhaps it took extra study and time to earn that high school diploma.

Perhaps you had to advocate fiercely for yourself to get the right diagnosis.

Perhaps you needed to suffer more pain in order to get through physical therapy and come out stronger.

Whatever the past achievements, they belong to us. No one can take them away, and no one can say we *can't* when we *did*.

So, if you did overcome great obstacles and achieve something awesome in the past, who is to say that you can't now?

It can be easy to forget the good in our past when present pain forces us to turn inward. One of the ways to be sure that past achievements are not forgotten is to have physical reminders of the successes visible in some way: a diploma framed and hanging on a wall at home, a picture that can be easily carried in a billfold, a journal that chronicles the events leading up to the achievement. Each of these things, and others, are ways to remember the good, even if it was laced through with difficulty.

From the past, we can glean joy in our accomplishments. In our present, we can embrace the many blessings, great and small, that God gives us each day and let them be as so many manifestations of God's love for us.

Most immediately, we have life, and that life gives us potential and opportunity.

We have unique and wonderful abilities that enable us to make contributions to the good of others. We have knowledge of good, and that can help us focus on positive, nurturing, more divine thoughts and activities so that we overcome the darkness of being drawn down by pain.

The person who says he or she has nothing to be thankful for just isn't looking hard enough!

✒ Into the Unknown

In our present, there is so much more than suffering. By reaching out to the blessings of the day, we are also extending our hands to God for support and strength, and in so doing, we are cultivating joy.

What do past accomplishments and present blessings have to do with seeing and believing beyond pain and the future? They can be powerful ways to believe without seeing the future clearly, and to *resolve* without necessarily understanding where that resolve will lead.

Did the disciples know that when they set out to spread the gospel, they would be sowing the seeds for what Christianity is today? No. Did they realize that because they infused in others the love and faith that they shared, some of them would be killed or imprisoned? No.

For the disciples, the future was unknown. But they knew the past—Jesus' ministry, miracles, and teachings. They knew the present—Jesus' resurrection and appearance to them. From these, they had the joy to be able to go ahead, beyond the confines of their homes and fears, and to witness.

If we believe that God has called us each by name and asked us to be lights for him, then we, too, are capable of going beyond what constrains us now. We can take our experience, achievements, and knowledge and help others who suffer. We can cultivate the blessings around us and make good in the world.

We can see our lives now as they are, and believe that God's desire for each of us is to live to our potential. We can bring out the joy that resides in us from all that is good and inspire more good, inside and out.

How exciting is that?

O Lord,
help me to never lose sight
of past achievements,
keep me always grateful
for present blessings.
Help me to replace my plaintive cries
with true thanks,
and bring me the courage to feel the joy
that is deep within,
and to bring that joy more fully to others.
Amen.

Others and You

*[Jesus said]: "This is my commandment:
love one another as I love you."*

JOHN 15:12

Relationships are very difficult to nurture and maintain when one person involved suffers chronic, overwhelming pain. Whether it is the relationship of parent to child, child to parent, spouse to spouse, or friend to friend, the emotional and physical toll that pain takes can prevent consistent, loving communication, and even rip apart what might have been strong bonds.

Yes, it is difficult to keep friendships, a marriage, collegial, or other relationships going if you live a life of pain. But it is crucial to find a way to do so. Not only are we called to reach out and love one another, but maintaining relationships with others enables us to focus on someone other than ourselves. In a very real, fundamental sense, when we serve others, care about and for others, and love others, we are serving, caring for and loving our Lord, too.

⋆ To Love Is to Give

Every so often, I receive an e-mail from someone who lives with horrible pain and who writes, "No one understands. No one cares. No one loves me."

On the surface, these communications stir my sympathy. Who among us has not felt loneliness at some time because of the isolation and unending onslaught of acute pain?

But as I consider what is behind the words of despair, I become a bit more practical, a bit more skeptical.

Is it really true that no one cares? No one at all? Not a relative, friend, physician, or stranger?

The truth is that, at this very moment, someone we do not know is praying for each of us. Somewhere in the world, at least one other person cares about us enough to include us in their communication with God. Strangers do care! They're praying right now.

Do physicians care?

To become a doctor takes years of specialized training, study, and sacrifice. These days, very few doctors become amazingly wealthy from their practice of medicine, and many age prematurely working more that twelve hours a day. Think of this, too: Doctors work with sick, despondent, angry people all day (rheumatologists, for example, treat people who cannot be cured and are constantly in pain). Could you do this and not care, fundamentally, about the work you do and the people you treat?

Relatives and friends hold a special place in our lives. Some, I will admit, are difficult to deal with. Some might even be toxic to us, abusive, or with addictive personalities that limit our ability to relate to them on an equal, reasonable footing.

But even if you have no living relatives and seldom see anyone you'd call a friend, in your past someone did care about you. Someone nurtured you, wiped your runny nose, taught you about life. We do not grow up in a vacuum. Someone gave us their time and attention, their care and love.

And herein lies the crux of what I think is the reason people lament not having anyone who cares in their lives: To care, to love, is to give of oneself. If we are so self-focused, so intent on demanding what we need and want, we do not allow anyone else the opportunity to express care for us. If we, in turn, do not care about or love others, we cannot expect that of anyone else.

🌿 Tend Your Garden

Nurturing people in our lives is much like tending a garden. We meet new people and begin new relationships (planting seeds). We engage with our friends and loved ones on a regular basis (weeding and watering). We recognize relationships that have limitations or are abusive and toxic and act appropriately (pruning). We find joy in the comfort and warmth that good relationships give us and in the service we can do for others (reaping the harvest).

A bountiful garden takes time, energy, and a sense of the needs of others. When leaves begin wilting, we look for the reasons and correct the situation. When seedlings need culling because there is not enough room to grow all of them in one space at one time, we do what's necessary.

Relationships thrive on mutual respect and love. Not every person in our lives needs a daily telephone call or e-mail. There are some friends we might correspond with only a couple of times a year, and yet these are strong relationships, too. But all relationships need our attention at some point.

🌿 The Power of Laughter

Some of my most precious relationships are with people with whom I can laugh. Not that we tell jokes. Sometimes our laughter is a quiet chuckle. Sometimes, it rolls on for minutes and bubbles up again after it subsides.

Laughter has physical benefits. It exercises our "core" and facial muscles. It releases positive hormones. It elevates mood. It brightens darkness.

Recently, some medical professionals have begun to study the positive effects of laughter on patients' ability to withstand difficult medical procedures or treatments such as chemotherapy.

Another benefit of laughter is that it can strengthen relationships. Once again, however, it is important to be able to see laughter and humor all around us and, sometimes, within us. We can best benefit from humor if we are willing to see the humor in our situation, life, and foibles.

Learning to laugh at ourselves is a fun way to go beyond the confines of pain.

I once received an e-mail from a man who criticized me for saying that laughter is a good way to cope with pain. He said that it physically hurt him to laugh, and because of that he'd decided that laughter was more harmful to him than good!

Truly, I beg to differ. A smile can uplift, even if a belly laugh is painful. And it can nurture a relationship in brighter, more encouraging ways than any litany of one's aches and pains could ever do.

Think You Can Do It All? Think again!

We cannot live alone, even if we might at times feel completely, physically alone. Yet, asking for help can be one of the greatest challenges of the pain sufferer. We don't want to "impose" on others. We are afraid that, by asking for help, we are showing weakness. We might fear that, if we ask someone for assistance, we're placing a burden on them that will break our friendship apart.

There might be people who will feel burdened by our requests. There might be some who will walk away. But, if you are the kind of person who hesitates to ask for help at all, or who insists that you're fine and in no need of assistance ever, I ask that you reconsider.

If we do not allow others who truly care to assist us, we are not letting them carry out their ministry of service to others. And if we refuse care, we are refusing to allow ourselves to be vessels for God's loving work.

Of course, if we are constantly calling on someone to do every little thing for us, we risk imposing too greatly. But, in my experience of working with patients who have lived with long-term pain, I find that the opposite is more of a problem. We who suffer try to do "it all," with the result that we stunt God's work.

We need to communicate with others if we want them to offer appropriate, effective assistance. We cannot expect that our loved ones will know what we need when we need it—unless we tell them. Our parents, spouses, children, and friends are not mind readers!

Remember, Job's friends sat around with him for days without speaking. They were so confounded and amazed at his downward spiral that they didn't know what to say, let alone do.

For the caregiver, it is always important to let your loved one know that you are there for him or her and willing to help.

For the sufferer, it is equally important to communicate your needs gently, lovingly, and clearly.

Breaking It Off

As difficult as it is to admit, some relationships are toxic and need to be either managed carefully or broken off. The last thing the pain sufferer needs is to be subjected to abuse, vitriol, and injustice. Yes, we are called to be of service to one another and to love one another. But we are also called to treasure the lives God has give us, and to care well for our bodies, even if they are racked with pain.

Some toxic people lack respect for us and for themselves, are abusive (verbally or physically), and sometimes try to draw us into their cycle of abuse, making us their victims. Other toxic people, by their personalities, lack of empathy, or other traits, sap us of our energy, patience, humor, or will to stand our ground.

In some cases, it is possible to build and maintain boundaries that respect your need for peace, care, and comfort, and keep a tangential contact with the toxic person. In other cases, especially if physical or psychological abuse is present, a more permanent, official intervention might be needed.

Breaking off a relationship can bring pain. But if it is necessary, if your safety is jeopardized, please seek help to bring you to safer, more peaceful ground.

⬥ Give and Take

In a good relationship, there is no score card of, "I did this for you and you did this for me." Yes, we are polite, thanking our friends and loved ones for the care they give. But we should not feel as if we have a tally sheet of items or favors given and received.

What we do need to be aware of, however, is that as much as we shouldn't have to feel alone, other people have responsibilities and pressures besides those we bring to them. We shouldn't feel rejected if a friend has a conflict with, say, the time of our doctor's appointment and so cannot provide us with transportation.

Just as we do not want every conversation we have with loved ones to be about our pain, so too should we be willing to offer our assistance, as much as we can, to those we care for and about. It's part of being a child of God, and part of being a friend.

⬥ Reaping the Benefits

As our gardens grow and blossom and yield fruit, we probably find ourselves seeing more clearly the flowers and trees and gardens all around us.

In the same way, as we have friends and are a friend, we reap wonderful benefits, and are able to "branch out" (pardon the pun) to encourage and pray for people more far-flung. We become part of the greater world, and one of those strangers who prays for people we do not know in places we've never been.

Through the recognition that we are not alone, never alone, we can send God's love far and wide—and feel the joy that comes from being a bright light glow ever more warmly within our souls.

Lord,

I know that with you I am never alone.

Help me to treasure the wonderful people

you have brought into my life.

Bring me greater wisdom to know

how I can be a better friend to those I know

and those I do not know.

And if it is necessary for me to build better boundaries

Or leave a relationship entirely,

please give me the strength and wisdom

to do the right and just thing.

In Jesus' name

Amen.

Good News of Great Joy!

Now there were shepherds in that region living in the fields and keeping the night watch over their flock. The angel of the Lord appeared to them and the glory of the Lord shone around them, and they were struck with great fear. The angel said to them, "Do not be afraid; for behold, I proclaim to you good news of great joy that will be for all the people. For today in the city of David a savior has been born for you who is Messiah and Lord"

LUKE 2:8-11

In their society, the shepherds were the lowest of the low. Great things didn't happen to shepherds. I can only imagine the terror the shepherds felt when an angel of the Lord appeared to them! How they must have been astonished at the angel's message of "good news" and "great joy!"

How their hearts must have been pounding when they traveled from their pastures to Bethlehem and beheld our Lord!

The lowly shepherds traveled from obscurity to the midst of the "greatest story ever told." From lives isolated and outcast, they were forever enveloped in God's love. From their simple work, they answered the call to be part of something amazing. And as they responded, their fear must have quickly fallen away and been replaced with awe and profound joy.

We who live with pain can often feel like outcasts, too. Living with pain can seem to us as if we are watching the world go by without feeling part of it. This isolation can settle deep within and bring on despair and depression—a far cry from joy.

Yet, even as we are set apart, all about us are manifestations of "good news" and "great joy." As we open our eyes, we see our surroundings— and God's gifts and call to use them, to "go beyond" our pain. Like the shepherds, we might tremble with fear at the thought of engaging in new activity. But the call remains.

How to answer it? How to discern just how we spend our precious energy in a way that God desires?

How to find our joy-filled purpose?

As we saw with Jesus' journey from Bethlehem to Calvary, purpose is not something static. It is the motivator that directs our steps and actions. Our Lord knew his purpose from the beginning and lived each day fulfilling it. He was driven, not by ego or personal gain, but rather by the desire to do his Father's work and to carry out his divine mission. He used the tools at hand, his talents and abilities, to fulfill his purpose, and he sought to inspire and teach others how to reap their heavenly reward.

For us to feel deep, abiding joy in our lives, we learn from our Lord that purpose is not something private and selfish. If we believe our purpose is to attain a certain degree of fame or status, or to amass a fortune, we are bound to be disappointed. These things might be gifts God bestows upon us, but we should not aspire to them as ends in themselves.

Rather, joy-nurturing purpose derives from taking off our selfish desires and putting on that which strives to reach out, lift up, and encourage. It is not measured in dollars earned or the number of accolades garnered. It is lived out daily, unfolding rather than defined in finite measurements.

Living a purpose is a lifelong process and is filled with surprises and detours. Each time we think we know how a particular part of our life is going to unfold, we realize that God might have other plans. If we resist, we will feel unsettled and pull back. If we accept God's way, we will sense a wholeness to our activities and lives—and joy.

Going forth into the world, even if it is onto the Internet from the sanctuary of home, can be scary. But what is the best way to overcome fear and acquire courage? It is by acting, by moving forward. Encouragement, prudent and prayerful choices, and a sense of humor are all part of being not afraid, and they are within the reach of each person who longs for a better life than the one lived in isolation with pain.

So, armed with Job's example, Jesus' inspiration, and a heart of courage, promise, dreams, and joy—what do we do now?

No matter how debilitated we are, what medications we must take, how many doctors we see, no matter how rich or poor, young or old— God has a unique purpose for each of us that rises above and goes beyond our pain and suffering.

Step by step, friend by friend, we build a life that embraces all that we are, including but not limited by pain.

We find ways to bring Light into the world.

We reach out to others who suffer.

We wake each morning with goals, and even if our health takes an unexpected turn, we know we have the strength to meet them sometime, if not that day.

We know ourselves so very much better than when we were pent in by pain.

We are more full of love than before.

I can't wait to see how the Lord works in our lives, now and forever!

Can you?

Lord,
I am ready.
Ready to answer your call.
Ready to take my pallet of suffering
and walk in your footsteps.
I understand that the way will not be easy,
nor will it be fast.
But with you guiding me, holding me,
and inspiring me,
I know all will be right.
Praise you, Lord,
For blessed am I who suffer!
You fill my heart with unending joy!
Amen.

JOY—FOOD FOR THOUGHT

Here are some questions to consider with others or on your own:

1. In what direction do you think God is leading you? Are you afraid? Eager? Ready?

2. Where is your favorite place to pray? How often do you go there? When could you find more time to go there?

3. What was the dearest dream of your childhood? What about it makes you smile today?

4. How complete is your belief in Jesus? Do you still ask him for tangible signs of his presence? How can you strengthen your belief?

5. What three things have you done for three friends this week?

6. Is there someone in your life who is toxic to you? Have you confided this to another friend? What does he or she think? How can you take steps to protect yourself?

7. When you hear good news, how do you react physically? Emotionally? What part of the Good News makes you react with this level of joy? How can you spread your joy to others?